Hatfield Answers the Call

1914 - 1919

Hatfield Volunteer Corps 1915

Written by Brian G Lawrence
Researched & Compiled by Christine & Derek Martindale

PUBLISHED BY HATFIELD LOCAL HISTORY SOCIETY

Hatfield Answers the Call
1914 – 1919

ISBN 978-0-9928416-3-8

Acknowledgements

Our thanks must go to the following organisations for allowing access to their archives and photographs: Mill Green Museum and Mill, Hertfordshire Archives and Local Studies, and Hatfield Library.

We would like to thank the following: Barbara Baker for information and photographs of Sgt. George Rice; Rosemary Marshall, daughter of Pte. Harry Ewington, for Harry's story and photographs; Janet Robinson for information about the Randall family; Ronald Addyman, curator of the Burton Salmon Millennium Exhibition, for the information and photograph of Pte. Thomas Bailiff, and the Marquess of Salisbury for allowing the reproduction of the picture of Viscount Cranborne, and for the photograph of the Rev. Lord William Cecil and his wife at the VAD hospital.

We would also like to thank Celia Gould for her meticulous work in correcting our errors and making the contents more consistent.

Lastly a special thank you to members of the Hatfield Local History Society for their support, and to the Hatfield Town Council for helping to fund this project.

Bibliography

1. Bishops Hatfield Parish Magazine, 1914-1922. (Held at Hatfield Library & St Etheldreda's Church, Hatfield)
2. Hatfield Parish Council Records, 1914-1922. CP44/29/26 & CP44/29/27 (Held at Hertfordshire Archives & Local Studies, County Hall, Hertford)
3. The Hatfield "In Memoriam & Roll of Honour Album", 1921
4. The Hertfordshire Advertiser, 1914-1918
5. Monumental Inscriptions of the Church of St Luke, Bishops Hatfield, Pt 1. (Hertfordshire Family History Society, 2009)
6. Tanks 1914-18. The Log-book of a Pioneer. By Lt. Colonel Sir Albert G. Stern, K.B.E. C.M.G. Hodder & Stoughton, 1919

Websites

1. Ancestry, Military War records, Census records and BMD records. http://www.ancestry.co.uk
2. Find my Past, 1911 Census Records. http://www.findmypast.co.uk
3. Commonwealth War Graves Commission (CWGC). http://www.cwgc.org
4. The Bedfordshire Army War Records. http://www.bedfordregiment.org.uk
5. The Canada Remembers Div. Veterans Affairs Canada. http://www.veterans.gc.ca www.collectionscanada.gc.ca www.canadaatwar.co
6. Forces War Records. http://www.forces-war-records.co.uk
7. Wikipedia. http://www.wikipedia.org
8. BBC. http://news.bbc.co.uk/
9. Imperial War Museum http://www/iwm/org/uk

Lt.-Colonel James Edward Hubert Gascoyne Cecil (The Rt. Honourable Marquess of Salisbury) commanded the 4th Beds. Batt. from 29 October 1892 to 8 January 1915, when he retired.

19th London Regt. Band Practice Hatfield 1914

Table of Contents

Troops entering Hatfield, 16 August 1914

**Dedicated to all those who served
The Survivors and the Fallen**

"Lest we Forget"

INTRODUCTION

The historical background to the outbreak of the First World War has been extensively debated and written about over many years and it is not appropriate to attempt to repeat here what has already been expressed more eloquently by earlier researchers.   Suffice it to say that for several decades before 1914 the storm clouds had been gathering over Europe, borne out of imperialism, a series of alliances and a feeling of a need for militarism on the part of several nations.   What is not in doubt is the fact that the assassination of Archduke Ferdinand of Austria by a Serbian nationalist in Sarajevo on 28 June lit the flame that engulfed the Continent within a few weeks.

From that fateful day at the end of June the general feeling was that it was not a question of **if** but **when** war would break out.   Once the stone had been thrown in the pond it was inevitable that the ripples would spread until they reached the furthest bank. Throughout July the major nations began to order mobilisation of their forces and on Tuesday 4 August, following Germany's invasion of Belgium, Britain declared war on Germany.   Lord Kitchener, the Secretary of State for War, at once appealed for the immediate enlistment of 100,000 men.   The famous poster showing Kitchener staring straight ahead, finger pointing and announcing "Your Country needs You" is still a compelling image and that, along with local recruitment drives in every city and town, instilled a tremendous sense of patriotism among the nation's young men. They were encouraged to take up arms and they responded in great numbers over the following weeks and months.   To qualify they were required to be not only fit for service and at least 18 years of age but it was laid down that they would not serve overseas until they reached the age of 19. It is apparent, however, that these age restrictions were often ignored with many recruits giving false names and ages in order to join up.   It is estimated that approximately a quarter of a million under-age boys were recruited and the records show that in certain cases boys as young as 15 years of age were killed on the Western Front. Two local lads who appear to have been among the under-age recruits were brothers, Alan and Gordon Stockbridge.   Though not born in Hatfield the family moved here when they were quite young and the boys were probably both working at Pryor Reid Brewery and living in the old town at the outbreak of war.   Records indicate that they enlisted in September 1914 as members of the Hertfordshire Regiment and gave their ages as 19, though they were just 17 and 16 respectively.   They were posted to France early in 1915 and both lost their lives on 18 May 1915, (at the Battle of Festubert), probably soon after the eighteenth birthday of Gordon, the older brother. Many of these boy soldiers were swept along by the overwhelming tide of patriotism but others were simply encouraged by their mates to enlist and saw this as an opportunity to experience some excitement and get away from their humdrum lives.

Festubert, after the battle.
Where Alan and Gordon Stockbridge lost their lives on
18 May 1915

We are given to understand that there was an early feeling of optimism on both sides that the conflict would soon be resolved and "it would be all over by Christmas" but it proved to be wildly inaccurate and the bitter conflict continued for more than four years. From the United Kingdom alone some 5.7 million men served in the forces during that period; over 700,000 were killed and over 2 million others were wounded. It is revealing to note that the total of enlisted men quoted is almost two million more than those who served in World War 2.

Recruiting Poster for the Herts Regt. designed by Mrs B.A.H. Goldie
(HALS)

Whilst we now have the overwhelming image of a national mood of optimism and patriotism, particularly in the early stages when there was a prevailing feeling that it would be a short-term conflict, it is certain that underlying doubts and tensions at all levels grew as the troops became bogged down and casualties rose. As the conflict dragged on into its second year with casualties continuing to rise, it became apparent that numbers could not be maintained at the required level merely by recruiting volunteers whilst at the same time maintaining a workforce to ensure that essential supplies were provided at home.

From the Bishops Hatfield Parish Magazine June 1915.
The 1st Herts Regiment.

On Saturday the 12th of June, a detachment of the 1st Herts Regt. Arrived in Hatfield for recruiting purposes. The District Council determined to give them a fitting reception and Mr Speaight, as Hon. Organising Secretary, arranged everything beautifully. A covered platform in the Broadway sheltered the District Council, headed by Sir William Church, Lord and Lady Salisbury, Sir E. Hildred Carlile and others. A Guard of Honour from the 1/10 County of London Regt lined the street, the Volunteer Corps, the Special Constables, the Fire Brigade and the Boy Scouts were much in evidence and a bevy of maidens with flowers greatly assisted the spectacular effect. . . . . of the five thousand inhabitants of our Parish no less than 361 have joined His Majesty's Forces, of whom over 100 enlisted in their County Regiment. . . . .eleven have had the honour of dying for their King and Country, one is prisoner, one is missing and 43 have been wounded. . . . . . We feel that there are others of our number who will respond to their Country's call.

The Recruiting Parade at the Broadway

The question of conscription became a contentious issue in Parliament as the months passed and by 1916 compulsory service was introduced. In his reminiscences, Harry Patch, who was to find fame much later in life as "The Last Fighting Tommy", related that he did not welcome the thought of war and was more interested in completing his apprenticeship. Nevertheless, when at the age of 18 he was called up he accepted that it was his duty to play his part.

Most of the images that we have grown up with as the decades have passed have focused on the men on the Western Front having to contend with fields of mud and damp, cold trenches but this was a war unlike any earlier conflict, stretching across the Continent and beyond. Thousands of men were deployed to the east in Gallipoli and the Middle East where they faced equally demanding conditions, including the extreme heat of summer, with flies covering everything in sight and bringing diseases such as dysentery and malaria.

Over 800 men from the town and surrounding villages that comprised the Hatfield District served during the war years. A high proportion of them served in the local Hertfordshire and Bedfordshire regiments with many others serving in regiments based in London and the Home Counties. Of course some would have been transferred between regiments according to demand as the war progressed but it is interesting to see the wide variety of regiments and other arms of the services in which local men served.

Among the regiments shown in the records are several Guards Regiments, the Northumberland Fusiliers, the North Lancashire Regiment, a number of Irish and Scottish regiments, at least one member of the Imperial Camel Corps and contrastingly another from the Tank Corps which came into existence during the war. The Royal Marines and the Royal Navy were also represented as were other recently formed units including the Royal Flying Corps, the Royal Naval Air Service and subsequently the Royal Air Force. Men who had previously emigrated, particularly those who had sought a new life in distant parts of the Empire, also rallied to the call. Such a case was Private William Davis, the son of Mr and Mrs Davis of 10 Primrose Cottages, Hatfield who had signed up in Canada. After coming to England in May 1916 he was drafted to France where he was killed in action on 17 September. The chaplain reported that he was buried on the battlefield but regrettably, owing to the confusion of shelling at the time, it was impossible to mark his grave.

**Pte. William Davis
Canadian Infantry 24th Bn.
K.I.A. on the Somme 1916.**
(*www.veterans.gc.ca*)

**The Grave of Peter Allan
Arnett, 27th Bn. 6th Brigade
2nd Canadian Division
St Luke's Churchyard**

Another Canadian who had only a very tenuous local connection but found his final resting place in Hatfield was nineteen year old Private Peter Arnett. He came over to England from Canada in the autumn of 1915 and after training was sent to the front in February 1916 where he was severely wounded in June of that year. He was brought back to England where he died in hospital in Orpington. Since he was the nephew of Mrs Allen, housekeeper at Hatfield House, his body was brought to Hatfield for burial. On arrival at the station the coffin was met by an escort of Royal Engineers and a firing party of 14 men and taken to the cemetery where a full military funeral was held, ending with the sounding of the last post by members of the Hatfield Troop of the Boy Scouts.

These are examples of bravery shown by men from the colonies who felt it right to volunteer to support their mother country. At the other extreme there were stories of conscientious objectors and we hear tales of white feathers being handed to men not in uniform suggesting, falsely in many cases, that they revealed nothing more than cowardice. Such incidents are unlikely to have been reported in the press at a time when a spirit of patriotism was very much the order of the day so it is not known if this practice was experienced locally. Of course there were many reasons why certain individuals did not qualify for military service and military tribunals were set up to access these cases once conscription was introduced in 1916.

Tribunals took place locally in the first instance but could then be referred to a higher county level and, if necessary, on to a Central Appeal Tribunal for Great Britain though it is apparent that this applied to only a small minority. (Lord Salisbury was appointed to the Central Appeal Tribunal for Great Britain in March 1916.) The main headings under which men may seek a tribunal hearing were categorised as fitness, personal hardship, business reasons or conscience. In order to prevent false accusations of cowardice, a medal, The Silver War Badge, was commissioned, which would show that the wearer had honourably fulfilled his duty to King and Country.

One Hatfield man to face such a tribunal was Hugh Lucy, a local butcher who appears to have been successful in obtaining several deferments, presumably on business grounds. However, his circumstances were submitted for a further review in January 1918. On this occasion he claimed that he was still able to get frozen meat and was the only butcher in the district who had any meat.   He presented a petition in support of his claim and sought a renewal of his exemption certificate.   His claim was questioned by the members of the tribunal and the decision was given that he must be called up within two months. Records show that he subsequently served in the Royal Naval Air Service and survived the war.

One of the most enduring stories of the early days of the war was that of the informal truce declared on Christmas Day 1914 when, it is said; British and German troops emerged from their trenches, exchanged greetings and played a game of football.   No record has been found of Hatfield men who took part in these exchanges but there are details of men from nearby towns and villages in Hertfordshire who wrote home giving information about incidents at the front where troops from both sides sang carols together, gave each other cigarettes and agreed to spend time in the no-man's-land between their trenches looking for their colleagues who had fallen in the fighting of previous days and giving them a proper burial.
Despite these 'local' truces the records show that 41 deaths took place on Christmas Day 1914 and significantly these informal truces and fraternisation were clearly a source of embarrassment to the military authorities.   This resulted in Commanding Officers issuing instructions that they were not to be repeated with the result that there were very few transgressions in 1915 and by the following year the overall animosity was so great that a truce was not contemplated.

Princess Mary's 1914 Christmas Gift

On Christmas Day 1914 everybody wearing the King's uniform and serving overseas was to be given this 'gift from the Nation'.   The box contained a combination of pipe, lighter, and cigarettes or for non-smokers a bullet pencil and a packet of sweets.

The 20th London Regt. on parade by St. Luke's

London Regt. 1914

THE LOCAL SCENE

Viscount Cranborne
*(Reproduced with kind permission of the
Marquess of Salisbury)*

In the summer months of 1914 Hatfield had been looking forward to the forthcoming celebrations, in August, to mark the coming of age of Viscount Cranborne, later to become the 5th Marquess of Salisbury. To mark the event it was decided to commission a nationally known artist, Arthur Cope (later Sir Arthur and a Royal Academician), to produce a portrait of the Viscount, and tenants, friends and neighbours of the Marquess of Salisbury were invited to contribute towards the cost. The celebrations were, not surprisingly, cancelled as a result of the crisis. In fact, the presentation of the portrait did not take place until 1920 and it was one of the official war artists, Sir William Orpen, KBE, RA, not Arthur Cope, who undertook the commission for a fee of £700. It is clear that the portrait was much appreciated by the Viscount who expressed his "cordial thanks" to all who had contributed towards the work.

Troops billeted at the Workhouse, Union Lane (Wellfield Road)

By the time war was declared on 4 August troops could already be seen in the streets of Hatfield. Members of a South London Territorial Unit, mainly from the Blackheath, Woolwich and Greenwich districts were there on summer training. Their tents were pitched in the fields adjacent to Briars Lane, near the site of the modern Swim Centre and their parade ground was on the present Asda car park. These men who became the 1/20 Battalion, The London Regiment, completed their training and embarked for France early in the spring of 1915 to be followed by a steady stream of men from the same regiment who were billeted in the town and underwent training in the surrounding countryside. The tented accommodation was merely a temporary measure and it was not long before the residents were urged to find room in their homes for this influx of soldiers. Most of the town's larger premises were soon brought into use as military accommodation including The Old Palace, The Riding School and Tennis Courts, the Reading Room and the Church Army Restroom and local schools. The Workhouse in Wellfield Road (then known as Union Lane) became their headquarters, and individual billets were found for the men in houses ranging from larger farmhouses to railwaymen's cottages in Gracemead and other long-established parts of the town including Glebeland and Fore Street. Several of the larger public houses also provided bulk accommodation. The "White Lion" housed some 60 men for much of the war. Apparently three officers took over the spare bedroom with another 50 or more other ranks finding shelter in the hayloft, skittle alley, stable, coach-house and woodshed. One of the soldiers later recalled spending his evenings in the "Robin Hood" playing a game called "Ringing the Bull" - a game at which only the landlord was proficient. Fifteen men were billeted above the Fire Engine House at a weekly rent of 17/6d.

The Fire Engine House

Soldiers billeted in Hatfield 1915

Inevitably the presence of troops in the town created extra demands on the local services. From the early stages the local Medical Officer for Health, Dr Lovell Drage was heavily involved in dealing with health issues including a number of outbreaks of scarlet fever among the soldiers. Another task that became part of the routine involved the cleaning of the various Billeting Stations which were also subject to regular inspections to ensure their suitability. The presence of soldiers billeted in schools was a cause of concern for the education authorities but it appears to have been resolved without undue disruption to the children's education.

20th London Regiment
December 1914, Christmas lunch at Hatfield

Indications are that the soldiers built up good relations with the local residents. In early 1915 the Rector, Canon Lord William Cecil opened a new YMCA Soldiers' Recreation Hut in French Horn Lane, described as a "substantial bright and airy structure" costing £300. In his speech he paid tribute to the soldiers in the town "whose behaviour had been without criticism". No doubt the Hatfield girls also welcomed the influx of soldiers, particularly as the local lads were going off to war, and there are several accounts of romances and marriages between local girls and soldiers from South London. A note on the back of a postcard sent by a soldier to a friend in New Cross provides an interesting picture of life at that time. It reads "*Had a 21 mile march yesterday morning - a teaser. By road it's 20 miles from Charing X to here. Could you cycle it next Sunday and have all day here? I'd love to see you old chivvy chum*". In June 1915 men of the 1st Herts Regiment and a band marched to Hatfield as part of a recruitment drive which included an open meeting and a church parade. The Lord Lieutenant of the County called for a census of males of military age in the district and although no figures were quoted, reports a few weeks later referred to "*a good number of local men recruited who were now on active service*".

The 20th Batt. London Regiment Hatfield 1914 (French Horn Lane)

In the early years of the twentieth century the three major employers in the town were Lord Salisbury's Estate, the Great Northern Railway and the Hatfield Brewery owned by Pryor Reid and Co. As more and more local men answered the call to arms the workforce of all these employers must have diminished and the firms concerned faced new pressures. With troops constantly arriving in the town for training, mainly those from the London Regiment, the station must have been much busier than normal at certain times while reduced manpower and resources would have made life more difficult on the Estate. At a very early stage it was noted that Lord Salisbury indicated that any of his horses would be made available though the hunters at Hatfield House were considered too light for military service. The House itself was made available to officers and other buildings such as the Old Palace, the Riding School and Tennis Courts were offered for the billeting of troops.

During the summer of 1915 some 900 men from the Royal Army Service Corps arrived at Hatfield, bringing with them 1500 mules. The mules were stabled in the Park and attracted a considerable amount of interest among the residents, particularly the children who made frequent visits to the Park during their stay. It is not recorded how long they remained there before presumably being transported to the front. However, a record of one incident that took place during their stay in the town has survived. This is a letter written by the Clerk to the Parish Council addressed to the commanding officer of the 11th Battalion of the County of London Regiment concerning one of the military mule vans which had damaged a street lamp near Gracemead Cottages. The Council felt obliged, therefore, to submit a claim for 7 shillings to cover the cost of repairs.

The 10th London Regt. entering Hatfield Park at the end of their route march passing by the statue of Lord Salisbury, 1914

20th Batt. London Regt. in Hatfield 1914

The 23ʳᵈ London Regt. marching past the Brewery entrance in the Great North Road on their arrival in Hatfield, 1915

The long-term effects on the Hatfield Brewery were even greater as, among the men who never returned, was Lieutenant Geoffrey Reid, only son of the Chairman of the long-established brewery, who fell at Ypres in 1915. When the brewery, based in the old town, finally closed in 1920 the Chairman stated that the loss of his son had led directly to this outcome. Sadly some brewery employees such as William Buck did not return but for those who survived it meant that they soon had to look for new employment. The other employers also lost staff at the front such as railwayman Conrad Austin who died of heat stroke in Mesopotamia, and Estate workers including George Currell, Robert Hall and Arthur Stallon.

Hatfield Brewery
Taken from the St James Review 1907.
The building covered much of the area now known as Salisbury Square.

Of course, it was not only the larger employers who were affected by the loss of experienced staff and in fact the impact on some of the smaller businesses and traders was probably even greater. Two well-established firms based in Park Street to suffer family losses were Mr Gregory, who ran a grocery business and Mr Richardson, a builder who each lost a son during the second half of the war.

As more and more men were called up so there was a greater demand for women to fill the gaps in the labour force. Some played their part by working on the land but others found themselves in jobs that previously would not have been considered appropriate for women. Waters Garage was given over to the production of munitions and a photograph

17

of the workforce taken outside the premises in 1918 includes some fifty females. It is interesting to note that the Chief Engineer was a Danish man Jens Christiansen who being classified as an alien had to report each morning to the police station before being allowed to start work on presumably products that were classified. A former Hatfield resident recalls other examples of women taking on men's jobs, such as Cissie Greene who became the local "dustman", a familiar figure riding through the streets seated on her dustcart.

Munitions Workers, Waters Garage 1918
Jens Christiansen, Chief Engineer, is leaning on the fence on the right of the photo.

Nurses at the VAD Hospital in the gardens of Northcotts with Dr. Lovell Drage

At the start of the war Mrs Seymour, the then commandant of the Hatfield VAD (Voluntary Aided Detachment), held classes at Hatfield House to improve the skills of its members. The Meeting Hall was designated to be an Emergency Hospital as it was the only large building not being occupied by the Territorials. In 1916 with increasing numbers of casualties, the Meeting Hall was replaced. The establishment of the VAD Hospital by the Red Cross, at Northcotts, just north of the gates to Hatfield Park, on the Great North Road was enthusiastically welcomed by the local community, particularly by Hatfield's women for whom it provided an opportunity to contribute something tangible to the war effort, especially for those who had been receiving training as part of the local initiative Northcotts, a substantial seventeenth century residence, had been occupied by the Military Authorities during the early part of the war but, in 1916, it was offered by Lord Salisbury as a hospital for sick and wounded servicemen. A team of supporters from the local Detachment quickly set about the task of adapting and preparing the premises for their new role and the efforts of local fund-raisers and generous donations ensured that the hospital was equipped to a high standard. It was formally opened by the Rector, the Rev. Lord William Gascoyne Cecil in the presence of the Marchioness of Salisbury, other members of the family and representatives of many local organisations, including the Girl Guides. Proceedings began with a service of hymns and prayers in the chapel of the hospital where the Commandant, Mrs W B Knobel, Quarter Master Mrs Bennett, Sister Hulm and the nursing staff, Mrs Baxter, Mrs Bishop, Miss Bury, Miss M. Caesar, Miss Church, Mrs H. Daniell, Miss Dewey, Miss Dunham, Mrs Ellingham, Mrs Gill, Mrs Gray, Miss Gray, Miss Hallows, Mrs Laing, Miss Russell, Miss G Seymour, Miss K Seymour, Miss M Seymour, Miss Forbes Tweedie, Mrs Vesey, Miss H Walker, Mrs Ward, Mrs Whincap, Miss Annie Bain, had assembled. There followed a tour of the building for the visitors who expressed their praise for the excellent manner in which the hospital had been fitted out. Staff accommodation on the first floor included a bedroom and sitting room for the Commandant, along with sleeping accommodation for the Sister and nurse in residence. The wards were well equipped and ready for use and there was a separate dining room and recreation room fitted out with couches, lounge and easy chairs, a piano, small billiard table and magazines and periodicals for the benefit of the patients. Dr. Lovell Drage was appointed physician and surgeon and within days of its opening the hospital was said to be "in full swing". The first patients to be treated at the hospital were 15 wounded soldiers, including several Canadians, who were transferred in from the Edmonton Military Hospital. The hospital soon became the focal point for much valuable local support work. This included a series of fund-raising concerts, a scheme of regular egg collections and monthly "Pound Days".

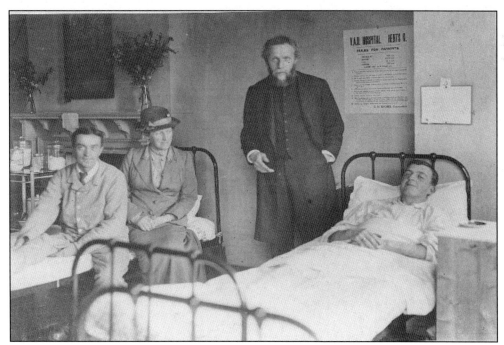

Rev. Lord William Cecil and Lady Florence
with patients at the Hatfield VAD hospital. *(Reproduced with kind permission of the Marquess of Salisbury)*

These special days were publicised locally and visitors to the hospital were then invited to bring with them goods, amounting to a pound in weight, to supplement the provisions offered to the patients.

Reports show that one of these Pound Days attracted over 200 visitors and the goods specially requested included eggs, sugar, tea, cocoa, jam and soap. It was noted that there were good supplies of tapioca and rice. Detailed records of the men who were treated at the hospital do not exist but it is known that one local soldier spent his final days there. This was George Rice of 8 Primrose Cottages (later Beaconsfield Road). He had spent much of his adult life in the army, having joined the Bedfordshire Regiment in 1886 at the age of eighteen, and served for twelve years before returning to civilian life and becoming a bricklayer. He re-enlisted in August 1914 with the rank of Sergeant and saw action on the Western Front. In August 1918 he was repatriated after suffering severe gas poisoning and died in the VAD hospital the following month. He left a widow and eight children and was buried in the cemetery at St Luke's Church. This is just one example of the valuable work undertaken by the staff and volunteers at Northcotts. The full worth of their contribution to the war effort cannot be assessed but it is known that a total of 790 patients were treated there before its closure on February 1919.

CWGC and family memorial to
Sgt. G. Rice
52268 Gloucestershire Regt.
3 September 1918

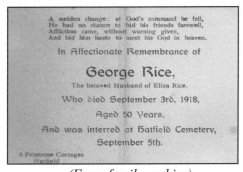

(From family archive)

Sgt. George Rice
(From family archive)

Hatfield Parish Magazine July 1916 VAD Hospital
The hospital goes well: all the beds are filled and preparations are being made to take even more patients; the numbers have already increased to 32, but more beds may be required as, since the Paris Push, the London Hospitals have been overflowing. The patients are mostly getting on well and seem to enjoy the comforts of the

Hospital. Mrs Minchin recently kindly provided a little entertainment for them at which Nurse Tweedie, Miss Hill and two sappers sang......

The following poem, composed by one of the patients in the months following its opening, clearly shows that the men who were being treated at the hospital appreciated the care and attention that they received from the staff and the local community.

"Pound Day"

You talk about hospitals and Convalescent Homes,
But I think Hatfield V.A.D. a splendid place to roam,
Our Matron, Sister, Nurses, have answered Duty's call,
Though their job ain't a picnic after all.

The people of this village will be very hard to beat,
For if you came on a Pound Day I'm sure you'd have a treat;
The presents they bestow on us are a credit to them all,
While I guess the Tommie's looking for another monthly call.

The Concerts they arrange for us is talent of the best,
I am sure our lads' behaviour has proved to them the rest:
Of course it's only natural for we (sic) their praise to sing,
Yet I hope there's no offence by the Soldiers of the King.

"A Tommy"

Royal Army Medical Corps. at Hatfield, 1914

Amid all this activity on the home front it must be remembered that 800 or more men from the town served in the armed services. In these days of instant communication it is easy to overlook the fact that they all left families at home anxiously awaiting spasmodic news from the front. Press reports show that it was not uncommon for wives and mothers to wait for weeks or even months to learn of the fate of their husbands and sons, and often it seems that the first news of casualties or losses received back home were letters sent by colleagues.

20th London Batt. at Hatfield 1915. Great fire near billet of Signallers

The Parish Magazine reported that on 11 November 1915 the Church Army Rest, a lodging house in Union Lane (Wellfield Road) close to the Workhouse, had suffered a fire which had completely burnt out the part of the building occupied by Mrs Stedman, the Superintendent. Fortunately soldiers were on hand to remove most of the contents and no injuries were suffered.

The precise location of the above photograph cannot be confirmed but the date on the photograph suggests that it could well have been the shell of the Church Army Rest.

FAMILY STORIES

William Johnson of Chantry Lane with his family c. 1916.
Sarah Ann Angell, Kathleen Allen (née Johnson), Florence Johnson (née Russell).
(Hatfield Library)

Though it is not easy for us, a hundred years later to envisage everyday life in the early years of the twentieth century there is no doubt that the effects of the Great War brought about changes to the lives of those who survived its horrors, both in this country and in many other parts of the world, that were greater than those experienced in any previous conflict. When the long-awaited peace returned and the troops returned home everyone realised that life would never be the same. Events as those experienced over the previous four years inevitably left their scars and showed no respect for status and reputation.

2nd Lt.
George E. Cecil
Killed in action
Villers Cotterets
September 1914

The town's most prominent family, the Cecils, suffered alongside the rest of the community. The 4th Marquess of Salisbury's brother, Lord Edward Cecil, lost his only son, George, during the first month of the War on 1 September whilst serving in France as a 2nd Lieutenant in the Grenadier Guards. Another of Lord Salisbury's brothers, Lord William Cecil, who had become Rector of Hatfield in 1888 and remained there until his appointment as Bishop of Exeter in 1916 shared with his parishioners the horrors of war. He and his wife, Lady Florence lost the first of their sons when Rupert, a Lieutenant in the 4th Bedfordshire Regiment fell at Ypres on 11 July 1915. On 1 December 1917 they lost their eldest son, Randle, a Lieutenant in the Royal Horse Artillery and then just six weeks before the armistice a third son, John, a Captain in the Royal Field Artillery, who had been awarded the MC was killed in action. Their loss is commemorated by the stained-glass window that was installed in the Parish Church soon after the war. It is said that the Rector burnt all the letters of condolence he received as they added so much to his suffering. Not only did Lord William and Lady Florence lose three of their four sons in the war but their one surviving son, Victor, was wounded on at least two occasions whilst on active service. If this was not enough, a few years later in 1924 they lost their youngest child, Anne. It was soon after this final tragedy that Lord William wrote:-

"Life must be taken as a whole, the sorrows and the joys. The mountain scenery is beautiful because the valleys are deep and the mountains are high. In life we are learning the beauty of God's creation. The

valleys are part, an essential part, of its beauty. They are dark, cold miserable: but taken with the mountains they make a glorious whole."

Having faced so many personal blows with such stoicism he was well-equipped to comfort his parishioners of Hatfield and later in the West Country when they faced similar tragedies during the conflict.

**Lt.
Rupert Edward
Gascoyne-Cecil
killed in action
Ypres,
July 1915**

**Lt.
Randle William
Gascoyne-Cecil
killed in action
Masnieres,
December 1917**

July 15th.

" . . . . . I was Lieut. Cecil's servant and was in his presence till five minutes before he was killed; he was hit in the head and passed away almost immediately. I must mention that your son will *always* be missed by us all, and we hope that you will accept our deepest sympathy. He was buried at Brigade Headquarters, about 1½ miles from where he was hit :· a wooden cross was placed on his grave with the following words inscribed :—

R.I.P.
Lt. R. E. G. Cecil,
1st Bedfordshire Regt.
Killed in action, July 11th, '15.

I must say that no one could wish to have a better officer than Lieut. Cecil. Several of us, including myself, were in his Company at Dovercourt. . . . . . .   Yours respectfully,
Pte. John A. Lawrence."

Extract from a letter published in the Bishops Hatfield Parish Magazine from Rupert Cecil's orderly

The following sequence of stories illustrates the stresses and strains experienced by many of the local families as they struggled to cope with the demands of everyday life in what was a closely-knit community in this small town.

Sgt. Harry Randall, DCM
(Mill Green Museum)

A long-established Hatfield family, the Randalls, was severely scarred by the effects of the War. Isaac Randall, lodge keeper at the main gate to Hatfield Park, whose wife died in October 1914 was left to face his family tragedies alone. His four sons all joined up in the early stages of the War. The eldest son, George Hayden saw service in France with the Royal Army Service Corps and survived the War. William Joseph who had been a Trumpeter in the Boer War, joined at the outbreak of war, was in the 1st Field Squadron, Royal Engineers and was killed in 1916. Charles Frank, a member of the Herts Constabulary, joined the Coldstream Guards, lost an arm whilst serving in France in September 1916 and was thus invalided out. He returned to the police service and ended his career as Deputy Chief Constable of Hertfordshire. The youngest son, Harry was a member of the Herts Territorials. He embarked for France in August 1914, was promoted to Sergeant in 1915 and was killed in action in April 1918. He was awarded the DCM and his citation reads:-

"For conspicuous gallantry and devotion to duty on March 22nd 1918 and on numerous occasions during the operation. He organised counter attacks with the utmost gallantry and led his men with amazing daring. Throughout the operations he behaved with the utmost courage. He led his men with great gallantry on 25th" (Extract from Special Brigade orders. 20 May 1918). Harry and William are both commemorated on the memorial in St Luke's Church.

Another wartime event that had lasting effects on the Randall family involved one of Isaac Randall's daughters, Helena Mary. Apparently her fiancé was killed in action and this led to her suffering a nervous breakdown. She never recovered from this and spent the remainder of her life in mental hospitals, firstly at Hill End and subsequently at Arlesey, Bedfordshire where she remained for some 40 years until her death in 1960.

The Hipgrave Family *(Herts Advertiser)*

As the war entered its fourth year in August 1917 the Herts Advertiser featured the story of the Hipgrave family from Roe Green, as related by Mrs Hipgrave. The account states that she had seen five of her sons and three grandsons answer the call to serve their country and illustrates the emotions that she must have suffered in the years that followed. Two of her sons had previously served in the Boer War from which they returned safely. They both joined the army again at the outbreak of the war and John was killed in December 1914, a month after being posted to France. William first went to France and then served in Egypt before being killed in Palestine in July 1917. A third son, Frederick, who joined at the same time, was killed in action in France in April 1915. Yet another of her sons, Frank was already serving as a corporal in India with the Border Regiment at the outbreak of war, having been in the army for some ten years. He was sent to the Dardanelles where he was wounded and after recovering was posted to France where he was wounded again. As a result of his wounds he was discharged at the age of 29 and returned to Roe Green. Mrs Hipgrave's remaining son, George, was wounded in France in April 1915, then served in Egypt and fortunately survived the war returning home to Roe Green where he lived with his wife.

It is difficult to imagine how families lived with this uncertainty constantly around them at a time when communications were so much slower than today's instantaneous news from the furthest parts of the world. This is vividly demonstrated in an extract from a letter sent to the Hipgrave family by a Company Quarter-Master Sergeant concerning the fate of William Hipgrave. It states that he had taken part in a night raid on the enemy trenches and had practically reached his bivouac when he was hit in the head by a stray bullet and died instantaneously. The letter goes on to express condolences to the family and to pay him the tribute of being a helpful and cheerful comrade who had died in the cause of his country and his loss was lamented by his colleagues of all ranks.

One of the Hipgrave grandsons, Private Charles Payne joined the 1st Hertfordshire Regiment early in 1916 and was killed in action in France in November of that year, aged 21. As he lived at Wymondley, near Stevenage he is not recorded on the Hatfield memorial. A second grandson, Private John Wilmot was already serving with the 1st Hertfordshire Regiment when war broke out and went to France in November 1914. Fortunately, as a 22-year-old, he returned home safely at the end of hostilities. Yet another grandson, George William Hipgrave, still a teenager, after serving in the navy as a Telegraphist on a destroyer, was also a survivor of the conflict.

From the diaries of the Bedfordshire Regiment in the Great War. *Second Umbrella Hill raid Gaza. All bar 2 of the men lost in the second raid were killed in the vicious hand to hand fighting in the Turkish trenches, and could not be recovered, hence have no known grave. 2 of the 9 Bedfords killed during the second raids against Umbrella Hill on the 27th July 1917 had won a Military Medal for their courage during the raids only a week earlier. Those killed in action that night were:*
201248 Private William Hipgrave *KIA 27/07/1917. Buried in Gaza War Cemetery. Son of Mrs. Elizabeth Hipgrave, of Roe Green, Hatfield, Herts. Born and resident of Hatfield, enlisted Hertford. His brother,* **4/6992 Corporal John Hipgrave** *was KIA 02/12/1914, aged 42 in the Bedfords in Flanders. He is buried in the RATION FARM MILITARY CEMETERY, LA CHAPELLE D'ARMENTIERES. His other brother* **4/7005 Private Frederick Hipgrave** *was KIA AT Hill 60 on 20/04/1915, serving in the 1st Bedfords in France, and is remembered on the YPRES (MENIN GATE) MEMORIAL.*

SERGT. H. STALLAN,
BEDS REGT.,
of Roe Green.
Awarded the D.C.M.

(Herts Advertiser)

The experiences of the Stallons illustrate once more the mixture of emotions that families experienced. Mr and Mrs H Stallon lived at New Cottages, Roe Green and their four sons and a son-in-law all served in France. The eldest son, Henry, of the Bedfordshire Regiment rose to the rank of Sergeant. His parents must have been proud to learn in May 1917 that he had been awarded the DCM for gallant conduct and devotion to duty in the field. The following year he was repatriated to this country after being wounded but fortunately he survived the war. His brother, Albert, died in Boulogne Hospital in October 1917, then William and Arthur were both killed in action in April 1918. The son-in-law, Driver Wood, was still serving in France in mid-1918 but it has not been possible to establish if he survived the war as he probably was not resident in Hatfield. It is difficult to imagine the grief that hung over this family as the parents followed events over the first three years and then suffered three devastating blows during the final year, two of which were just weeks apart in the spring of 1918.

Sadly the family of Mrs Currell of Green Lane Cottage, Hatfield also paid a high price for their contribution to the war effort. Son John who had previously been awarded the Military Medal was killed in action on the Western Front in September 1916. Another son, George, who had worked on the Estate in Hatfield Park, served in France where he was killed in action just a week before the armistice. Fortunately a third son, William who had been employed on the farm at Harpsfield Hall survived the war though by 1917 he had been wounded twice and been repatriated to a hospital in Norfolk.

Mr and Mrs G Nash who lived in Primrose Cottages during the war years must have breathed a sigh of relief when the conflict finally ended. Their three sons all served in the forces and although two of them returned home bearing the scars of war, unlike so many other families, they were eventually reunited. The oldest son, George William of the Bedfordshire Regiment joined the colours early in 1916 and after initial training in Kent was sent to France where he suffered wounds to his leg and arm after a few months at the front. His younger brother, David Edward enlisted a year earlier and spent time in India and Mesopotamia. He had two spells in hospital suffering from fever but was able to return to his battery in 1917. The youngest brother, Thomas, was undoubtedly keen to emulate his older brothers and in the early months of 1917, at the age of just 16, was serving as a bugler in the Herts Volunteers' Regimental Band. He is almost certainly one of the two men of that name listed on the roll of honour of Hatfield men who served, although the regiment quoted alongside the name is different

THE BROTHERS NASH.

(Herts Advertiser)

George Lawrence and his wife, Ann, of Beaconsfield Road, near neighbours of the Nash family, said farewell to their four sons as they all headed off to join the forces during the first few weeks of the war but over the following four years they must have suffered periods of great anxiety and were left with scars that remained with them for the rest of their lives. The eldest son, George, had served as a member of the 1st Herts Territorial Force before signing on as a member of the 75th Canadian Infantry but was killed in action in France in June 1917. His brother, Thomas, another member of the Herts Territorials, joined the same Canadian regiment and at the time of George's death had been posted as missing though, in fact, he had been killed in action some three months before his brother. The two younger brothers, William of the 1st Hertfordshire Regiment and Herbert, a Signaller with the 8th Bedfordshire Regiment, both survived but neither was unscathed. William was wounded whilst in France and Herbert returned suffering from shell shock.

George Lawrence   **Thomas Lawrence**
(www.veterans.gc.ca)

One particular household on the outskirts of the district, at Ponsbourne Park, Newgate Street, that had experienced considerable grief even before the war was to continue suffering throughout the years of conflict. Charles and Hetty Speller lost two of their seven children at an early age then lost all four of their remaining sons during the war years. Three of the boys were either in the forces by the time war broke out or enlisted during the early days. The war was less than three months old when Augustus Charles was killed in action in October 1914. His brother, Herbert James, was also killed in action on the

**CWG of
Leonard Walter Speller
Gunner, Royal Field
Artillery
Died 5 June 1918
St Mary's Churchyard
Ponsbourne/Newgate St.**

Somme in November 1916, followed by another brother, Walter John who died in action in October 1917. Finally the fourth son Leonard Walter was severely injured whilst training at Shoeburyness, Kent, the Royal Artillery training base. He died from his wounds a few days later in June 1918, just as the war approached its final phase and is buried in St Mary's Churchyard Ponsbourne, Newgate Street.

Undoubtedly most of the stories of the exploits of Hatfield's men involved those in the army battling with the muddy conditions they encountered in France and Belgium or in the heat of the Middle East, but there were others who played their part in the air or on the high seas. One whose dramatic story took place in the Mediterranean was Walter Skeggs whose home was at Stanborough. On 4 May, 1917 he had been serving for 16 months as a member of the crew of the Cunard Liner Transylvania, when the ship was torpedoed by a German submarine. Young

Cunard Liner Transylvania
Sunk by German U-boat U-63, May 4 1917,
(Wikipedia)

Walter was on watch at the time and assisted in lowering the boats and rafts until he was thrown into the water. He was eventually picked up after struggling to remain afloat there for some three hours and fortunately lived to tell the tale. At the time he had three brothers all serving in France and happily the records suggest that they all survived the war.

The dramatic events of 31 July 1917, as the Third Battle of Ypres was raging in the vicinity of Passchendaele, cast a dark shadow over four particular households in the district. It was on that very day that four local lads were killed in action at St. Julien. They were Lance Corporal John Coe, Private James Day, Private Robert Putterill and Corporal George Victor Webster. Three of them are commemorated at the Menin Gate Memorial whilst Corporal Webster was buried at Buffs Road Cemetery. Their names also appear on local memorials, James Day on the Ponsbourne and Newgate Street Memorial and the remaining three on the Hatfield Memorial. Reports of the fierce fighting that was taking place at the height of the battle reveal that one of the men was killed as he carried out his duties as a stretcher bearer. Another had

**The road from St. Julien to Ypres during the Third
Battle of Ypres.
Taken on the first day (31 July 1917) by the 13th
Royal Sussex**

volunteered for this dangerous assignment at the front to relieve a colleague who had a large family and the third, Victor Webster, who had served for almost three years, having enlisted in October 1914, was fatally injured as he brought his gun team into action.

620 men of the 1st Battalion of the Hertfordshire Regiment took part in the Battle of St. Julien, attacking the German trenches on that morning but after two hours fewer than 100 of the men returned, the rest having been mown down by machine gun and artillery fire. Thus, it is recorded as the most devastating day in the county's military history. As the centenary of this tragic event approaches a programme is being

launched within the county to commemorate this local sacrifice. The plan is to raise funds and install a memorial at the site of the battle exactly 100 hundred years after the event. It is hoped that the ceremony will take place in the company of descendants of the men lost in the battle and the few of those who survived.

Another poignant story concerns Acting Bombardier Frank Mardle of the Royal Field Artillery, son of Mrs Mardle of Cromer Hyde. The account of his death on 11 June 1916 states that his Battery had been engaged on a part of the front that had experienced ceaseless fighting for the past fortnight. It would appear that as he was firing his gun a shell burst with pieces cascading in all directions and he was killed instantaneously. The Commanding Officer paid tribute to him as an efficient and well-liked NCO who died doing his duty. He assured Mrs Mardle that her son had been buried close to the battery and his colleagues had marked his grave with a cross. What made this story particularly distressing is the fact that on the day his mother received the sad news the family received a letter from Frank himself in which he describes the action of the previous few days. His graphic account of the action includes the following quote:-

"Fritz started shelling our trenches about nine o'clock last Friday morning and from (then) until about midnight Sunday we were at it night and day. In fact we have not had a decent sleep since, as we have had to replenish our ammunition store in readiness for another attack. We were firing so fast that ammunition had to be brought up in daylight and Fritz was shelling the roads heavily at the time. The shells fell all round us but luckily nobody at the guns was hit. We had two direct on our pit but were so busy sending them over we took no notice at the time. The guns got so hot that the paint peeled off the muzzle. The Germans got into our frontline trenches, but suffered very heavy losses in doing so. Fritz paid very dearly for the little ground he gained and we are still worrying him. I am expecting to be relieved for a rest at the week-end but would rather stay here if there is anything doing."

These words probably sum up the character of the man better than any tribute could hope to convey. It was not, however, the end of the family's suffering as Frank's elder brother was killed in action in February 1918.

Pte. Harry Ewington
10th Rifle Brigade
(Family archive)

The following extracts from the diaries and letters sent by Harry Ewington to his young wife and family back home in Hatfield provide a rare, first-hand insight into his thoughts and experiences of life on the frontline. Harry, son of an engine driver, spent his early years living in Gracemead Cottages and was employed by Tingeys for the vast majority of his working life, initially as a grocery boy. He joined the 10th Bedfordshire Rifle Brigade in May 1916 and spent some weeks at Ampthill Camp before undertaking further training at Felixstowe prior to embarkation for France. By October he was on active service and in a letter to his young wife he described the harsh conditions in the trenches with remarks such as *"this job will make a man of me if I get through ... it broadens the mind a bit"*. A machine gun course was something of a culture shock to him and the range of food available must have been a sharp contrast to that which he had been delivering around Hatfield and the surrounding villages. On one occasion, unable to find a mug for his tea, he resorted to buying a tin of pineapple in order to have something from which he could drink his tea but there were occasional treats such as Melon and Ginger jam from Australia.

Harry in France   Marriage to Edith
(Family archive)

As winter approached conditions became worse and his spirits were kept up by the regular parcels sent by his wife and mother. The range of goods packed into these parcels is quite revealing as they included tins of fruit, cake, chocolate, fresh fruit and even sausages, veal pie and on at least one occasion a fresh chicken. Clothing was also in short supply so pleas were made for socks, gloves, underwear and even a pair of boots. These were readily sent, along with small amount of English money which apparently could be used to buy eggs and milk from local French farms. His wife and family never failed to meet his requests which undoubtedly added to their own difficulties bearing in mind the shortages that were being experienced back home.

Harry's letters invariably struck a positive note concerning his own state of health with comments that he was keeping fit *"trotting after Fritz"*. In keeping up his spirits he must have been helped by his strong Christian faith, demonstrated by the fact that he regularly mentioned the Sunday Church Services

Harry's Medals
(Family archive)

frequently held in a barn or under a hedgerow – a refreshing change from life in the trenches. Images of troops trudging through the mud in winter are widely known but it is apparent that these conditions could persist well into the summer as he described his boots full of water while he slept in a leaking barn in mid-July. His diary vividly tells of an attack when a shell burst within fifteen yards of their position, killing one of his pals. He goes on to say *"I nearly got a blighty"* adding that a piece of shrapnel pierced his helmet but glanced off without injuring him. However, the fierce fighting continued and within a month his luck ran out and Harry's war was over. He suffered severe stomach wounds and was taken to a nearby hospital. Raids on the hospital meant that he had to be moved to a casualty station, then on by train to Rouen before being repatriated to Uplands Hospital in Winchester where, due to his serious injuries, he spent several months. As in so many cases at that time his wife experienced several weeks of anxiety before she received any detailed information of his injuries or whereabouts. Once he had begun to make progress his wife and other family members were able to make the long journey to Winchester to visit him.

Following his discharge from hospital Harry was invalided out of the forces in January 1918 and apparently was told that he may have only a year to live but happily this was not so. He continued to make steady progress and in due course returned to work for the Tingey family.

When their new furniture store was built after the war he transferred to that side of the business and lived with his wife in a new house built alongside the store at the junction of St Albans Road and French Horn Lane. He became the manager of Tingey's furniture department and continued to work for the firm well into his seventies. It is pleasing to report that he defied all the medical predictions and was able to provide loyal service to his employers and the local community for so long until his death at the age of ninety in 1976.

Three sons of Mr and Mrs Parrott of Salisbury Square gave their lives for their country. The first son to die was William John who died of wounds in this country. The following is an account, from the Herts Advertiser 26.6.1915., of his funeral in Hatfield :–

Sapper William John Parrot, of the 173 Company of the Royal Engineers, whose home is in New Town, Hatfield, was so badly wounded during the repairing of the trenches on Hill 60 that after lingering on for some time in St Thomas's Hospital, London, he died on June 6th. He leaves a widow and four children. He was buried with full military honours at Hatfield by the 1/11 Battalion London Regiment. The cortege moved off from Hatfield Station at 1.30 in the following order: - The Firing Party under Sergt.

PTE. W. J. PARROT
(HATFIELD).
of the 1st Bedfordshire Regiment, who died from wounds in St. Thomas's Hospital, London.

(Herts Advertiser)

Carter, the Band and bugles, under Bugle Major Rose: and a large detachment under Sergt. Sayer. The Band rendered during the march to the church the "Dead March" in "Saul" and the hymn tune "Abide with me". Then followed the coffin with eight pall-bearers, and mourners. Mrs Parrot (widow) was supported by Mr G Parrot (brother), deceased's mother and father, Mr and Mrs Bert Parrot, Pte Charles Parrot of the 1st Herts Regt., Mr Farmer, Mrs G Parrot, Mr and Mrs Tyler, Mrs Littlechild, Mrs Overington, and a few other close friends. The route from the station to the cemetery was lined with friends and members of the 1/10th London and 1/11th London Regiments. Upon reaching the church, Canon the Rev. Lord William Gascoyne-Cecil M A held a short service, assisted by the Rev. G F Baxter, M A. The procession was then re-formed for the last journey to the grave. The Rev. Lord William Cecil carried out the last rites, delivering a short address to the mourners, which was followed by three shots being fired over the grave by the firing party and the "Last Post" was sounded by the buglers of the 1/11th London Regt. There was a wreath in the form of a large glass globe through the efforts of Mrs Lawrence – Mrs W J Parrot and the family hope that all kind friends will accept their heartfelt thanks for the great kindness and sympathy shown to them during their bereavement.

Frederick Arthur Parrott of the Sherwood Foresters, Notts. & Derby regiment, was killed in action on the 4 October 1916 and is buried at Bellacourt Military Cemetery, Riviere. Herbert James Parrott of the Machine Gun Regiment was also killed in action on the 2nd July 1917 and is buried at St. Vast Post Military Cemetery.

Bridge building across the river Lee

Bridge built over the river Lee by the 11th London Regt.

SPORT, SOCIAL & COMMUNITY ACTIVITIES

Before a football match
Hatfield Park

For most of the population life was hard during the early years of the twentieth century. Work was physically demanding, hours were long and the opportunities for leisure were fewer and less varied than they are today. Nevertheless the working man valued his leisure time whether it was spent in the local hostelry or on the sports field. Of course, it was inevitable that when the men began to depart for the front many aspects of "normal" life were under threat. As now, football was then an important leisure activity for many of the population and men throughout the country would have been looking forward to the opening of a new season when the hostilities began. Unfortunately organised sporting competitions were disrupted, the Football Association suspended league and cup competitions for the duration of the war and locally county football competitions were abandoned by early 1915.

Later that year it was reported that 59 members of Hatfield United Football Club had "answered the country's call" and two had been killed at that early stage. It is not possible to give an accurate assessment of the many keen and able sportsmen from the district whose sporting careers were cut short by the war. Among those who did not return were men like Harry Gregory, son of the Park Street grocer, described as a talented humorous vocalist, and a local cricketer, footballer and tennis player who was killed in France in 1917. Another was Lt. Patrick Caesar, whose family lived at Galleycroft, on the site of the present Swim Centre. He had been studying at Oxford University and was planning to take Holy Orders before the war, having been closely involved in social and church work in the parish, as well as being a prominent cricketer. These are just a couple of examples but there must have been many more cases like these plus those who did return but had suffered lasting injuries which would have brought their sporting careers to an abrupt end.

Pte. Henry Gregory
Hon. Royal Artillery
Comp.
killed in action
8 February 1917
(Mill Green Museum)

Fortunately there were others who had to suspend their local activities for the time being but were able to return and play their part in rebuilding the social life of the town later. Two of these were William Groom and Billy Watson. William Groom, who had worked on the Estate, was an accomplished racquets player and a leading member in the Cricket Club. He distinguished himself

33

by his "conspicuous bravery in the field" and was awarded the Military Medal. Billy Watson was a key member of both the Football and Cricket Clubs and was reported missing in March 1918. The following months must have been an extremely worrying time for his wife and family but after two months Mrs Watson received official notification and a card from her husband to say that although wounded he was then a prisoner of war. The timing of his return home is not known but he threw himself back into local life and for many years thereafter he served as Secretary and Treasurer of the Herts Football Association, became the county's representative on the English Football Association and was made a Vice-President of the English FA in recognition of his services to the game.

Whilst much of the regular sporting calendar was abandoned it did not mean that sporting activity came to a complete halt. Whilst these informal fixtures were rarely reported in the way that organised matches would have been eagerly read in peacetime, it was only natural that local civilian lads would take any opportunity to relax in this way either amongst themselves or by arranging some form of competition against soldiers who were stationed in the town, either as part of their training or on special assignments. Photographs taken in the Park show members of the Royal Engineers in their full football kit with a ball at their feet.

Royal Engineers Football Team, Hatfield Park
(This photograph appears to have been taken in the area now called Stable Yard)

One Football match which managed to get coverage in the local weekly newspaper along with a team photograph was played in Mesopotamia between troops of the 1st and 2nd D Squadron of the Herts Yeomanry. Apparently the match resulted in a win by one goal to nil for the 1st squadron and Lieutenant Cecil Bury of Hatfield played at left back for the winning team. The report of the match adds that it took place in the evening and was limited to half an hour each way due to the heat. Fortunately Lieutenant Bury was among the survivors of the war, during which he won the Military Cross and was promoted to the rank of captain.

There are a few details of cricket matches being played locally, probably in the Park, during the war years. These include matches between a Hatfield team and 1/10 County of London Regiment and also an inter-service game between another team from the County of London Regiment and 1/5 Bedfordshire Regiment. A team from the Royal Engineers later took on a Hatfield team but unfortunately no information remains as to the outcome of these matches.

Whilst sport continued to be important in keeping up the spirits of residents and troops as they prepared to face more serious opposition, the social and community life of the town assumed even greater significance.

The 23rd London Regt. passing the entrance to the Public Hall, Great North Road
(centre right with Cinema in bold lettering across the top.
The Great Northern Public House can be seen centre left)

The small town of Hatfield had a well-established social life with numerous clubs, many pubs and beer-houses scattered around the streets of both the old town and the growing settlement along the St Albans Road, known as Newtown.   However, a more recent centre of community life had become the focus of attention with the opening of the new Public Hall, off the Great North Road, in 1911.   Throughout the war years the Public Hall was a popular venue for meetings, concerts and plays, often prompted by members of Lord Salisbury's family or other prominent citizens, designed to boost the spirits of the residents and the constant stream of military personnel who were billeted in the town.

From the earliest days of the war there was a realisation throughout the land that fund-raising would become a priority if Britain were to be victorious.   This led to a rapid increase in the number of flag days for a wide variety of causes from Belgian Refugees or the Serbian Relief Fund in the early days, on to Wounded Soldiers and Shipwrecked Mariners and later to Prisoners of War.   These flag days were often street collections organised nationally but more local initiatives were equally important.   Within less than a month of the outbreak of war the first of a series of Smoking Concerts for the Troops was held in the Public Hall which had also become a Reading Room by that time.   This set the tone for many more concerts which enabled the residents to demonstrate their support and feel more involved with friends and family serving at the front.   Typical of these concerts was one organised by Lady Salisbury which raised money for the Fund for Sick and Wounded at the Front in September

1915.   With the opening of the local VAD Hospital in 1916 a considerable amount of the activity was directed towards the running of the hospital and the wounded soldiers who were being treated there. Events at the Public Hall included a concert given by a group known as the "Hatfield Patriots" and a musical play entitled "The Wood Nymphs" which played to two full houses.   These performances raised funds for the hospital, the local branch of the Red Cross and the Hatfield Nursing Association.   Another intriguing fund-raising activity held there was a "Fag Concert" given by the nurses and wounded soldiers, admission by a shilling's worth of fags, which provided over 3000 cigarettes for wounded soldiers.

Whilst the Public Hall was the focal point for much of the local fund-raising activity the summer months provided other outdoor opportunities such as the military tattoo held in the Broadway featuring the Bugle Band of the 3rd Battalion of the Herts Volunteer Reserve and the first performance by the Hatfield Town Band. The latter had been practising under Bandmaster Posey and "acquitted themselves admirably", attracting a large audience who thoroughly enjoyed the musical evening.

Just to show the folk back home that the lads at the front were also doing what they could to keep their spirits up the Herts Advertiser published a photograph in August 1916 of the Herts Band in France which included men from across the County and two local Hatfield men, Drummer R. Hall and Drummer A. Greenham. Unfortunately Private Robert Hall was killed in action in France in 1918 but Private Arthur Greenham was among those who returned home at the end of hostilities.

Hatfield men, Drummer Robert Hall & Drummer Arthur Greenham are the two men standing in the middle of the top row *(Herts Advertiser)*

Equally important was the need to maintain the community feeling involved in the common cause and this is demonstrated in a letter written by Alfred Whitby, Clerk to the Parish Council in July 1917 when every snippet of good news from the front was soon offset by another setback. Mr Whitby's letter was addressed to Lord Hugh Cecil the bachelor youngest brother of the Marquis of Salisbury. He explained to him that at the suggestion of the Lord Lieutenant the Council had decided to organise a Public Meeting at the Public Hall on the evening of 4 August. The meeting would be chaired by Sir W. J. Church and the following resolution would be submitted:- *"that at this the third anniversary of the declaration of a righteous war, this meeting records its inflexible determination to continue to a victorious end the struggle in maintenance of those ideals of Liberty and Justice which are the common cause of the Allies".*

No further reference to the meeting has been found but there seems little doubt that such a motion would receive the unanimous support of everyone present.

It is entirely understandable that the Council would seek the involvement of the town's leading family in rallying the support of the whole community at this bleak time but why they should focus particularly on Lord Hugh Cecil is somewhat less clear. In his book on *The Cecil's of Hatfield House*, Lord Hugh's nephew, the famous historian, Lord David Cecil writes of his uncle:-

"From the beginning my uncle hated the war and especially when it led to the introduction of military conscription, which he looked on as perhaps inevitable but a disastrous blow to the sacred cause of individual liberty. Himself, he believed the war to be justified and proceeded to join the Air Force: a gesture heroic but comical, for no one had less gift for operating any kind of machine. The Air Force recognized this and, after he had managed shakily to pass his first flying test, found work for him on the ground. Joining the forces did not change his principles. He got special leave from the Air Force to go and make an impassioned speech in the House of Commons in defence of the right of conscientious objectors to act as their individual consciences dictated."

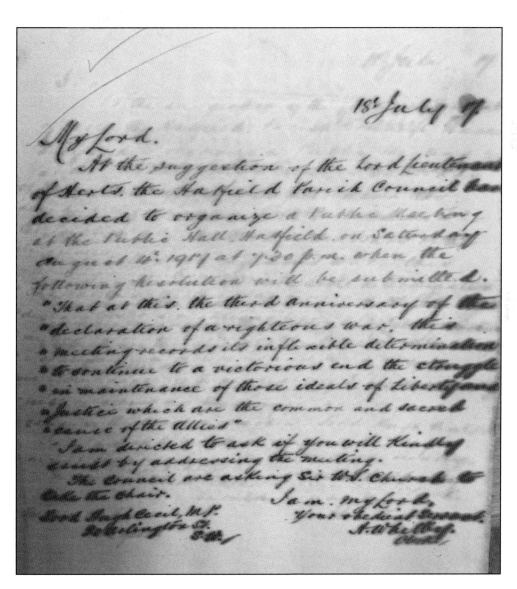

**Carbon copy of the letter sent to Lord Hugh Cecil from
Alfred Whitby, Clerk to the Parish Council
July 1917**
(HALS)

(Copy)

West Goldings,

Hatfield.   22 August 1917.

Local Food Control.

The Hatfield Rural District Council,

Gentlemen,

On August 9th, I received a letter from Mr. Dunham stating that the District Council had agreed to offer me the position of Food Inspector, I replied the same date saying that I should be pleased to accept the position and thanking the Council for the appointment. I saw the Clerk to the Council the following morning and he supplied me with a number of circulars on the food question which I went through, and commenced my duties at once.

I have visited every Bakers' Shop in the Rural District and made full enquiries into their mode of making bread, the time given before exposing it for sale etc, and in every case I was assured that the regulations were being strictly carried out, I tested the weight of the loaves at every shop and with one exception I found each shop loaf full weight, two loaves I tested at Mr.Jessops, Park Street, Hatfield, were a trifle below two pounds, but only just a trifle-, I told the person in charge to remedy the matter at once, and on paying a second visit I found the loaves full weight. There are only two Bakers in the whole district who make confectionery namely Messrs Hill & Son, and Mrs.Thomas, both of Fore Street, Hatfield, and I have every reason to assume from the enquiries I made that

Appointment of the Food Inspector *(HALS)*

SUPPLIES, SHORTAGES & RATIONING

WW1 Information Poster
(Imperial War Museum)

As soon as war was declared and the first of the men began to enlist, appeals went out to provide supplies that would be necessary to support the war effort. The Government warned the public that raw materials that came in large quantities from Germany and Austria would soon be in short supply and alternatives would need to be sought.

The authorities were very conscious that the effects of shortages would soon begin to be felt in homes throughout the country but were anxious not to create panic or lower the spirits of the population. In the early days of 1915 a report was published in the local press under the heading "A Word from the German Hausfrau". It highlighted the fact that the women of Germany were looking forward with anxiety and apprehension to the coming winter months. The price of the more necessary provisions such as bread had increased appreciably and the German government was accused of allowing prices to rise in the "wildest disorder" as a result of which women were having to fight against privation in Berlin and other cities. This was contrasted with the state of affairs at home where women should be reassured to know that due to the steps taken by the British government and the strength of the British Navy and Army there was very little increase in the price of ordinary provisions.

As the war dragged on into its second year it was felt appropriate to provide guidance to motorists to ensure that the wheels on their vehicles were correctly aligned so that wear on tyres was reduced. Drivers were also urged to slow down when passing marching soldiers so that they did not stir up dust and to avoid coast roads where lights were not permitted. This was not relevant in this part of the country, of course, but in some other parts it was feared that any lights might alert enemy shipping that happened to be close to our coastal waters. At about this time the government announced that there would have to be an increase in the price of petrol sold to the public to 1/10d (approx. 9p) per gallon. It seems unlikely that this would have a direct effect on most of the population but it was felt that the authorities should try to demonstrate that the British public were appreciably better off than the Germans as they also made it clear that petrol over there had increased to 4/9d (almost 24p) per gallon.

With more and more men being sent to the front efforts were being made to encourage women workers on the land. In April 1916 Lady Salisbury was among the speakers at a meeting held in Hitchin Corn Exchange where it was announced that within the county 1000 women had so far taken up full-time work on the land with another 1300 working on a part-time basis. It was stressed that it was not "infra dig" for women to be employed on the land at this time when food supplies were so essential and it was proposed that they should work in gangs with a forewoman to supervise and keep time-sheets. At about the same time, as part of a county scheme, the Hatfield Women's Agricultural Committee was formed to promote this initiative with Lady Salisbury very much at the fore stressing the need for local women to support the men who had left the land to fight for their country and urging them to make their services available to local farmers, even if it could be for only a few hours a week, to secure food for the country at such a crucial time. Subsequent reports indicated that this appeal had proved to be very successful.

(Imperial War Museum)

It is apparent from reports that throughout the country provisions were becoming stretched, particularly as there was a wide-spread shortage of eggs and poultry, and at the end of 1916 Lady Salisbury sought to tackle this problem by arranging a series of three lectures by a well-known poultry expert, at the Public Hall, admission free.

Whilst these measures undoubtedly proved effective in maintaining supplies the women alone could not provide the complete answer as many women were covering an increasing diversity of roles as time went by. Eventually further steps had to be taken to tackle the acute need to boost local food production. In the summer of 1917 the Rural District Council decided to appoint an inspector under the Food Controllers' Orders and the post was filled by Mr H. Pritchard. One of his first jobs was to visit the town's bakers to ensure that the loaves they produced were of "full weight". He made regular checks to ensure that firms were using their sugar allocation for the correct purposes and that retailers displayed the correct prices for the sale of goods including meat, milk and tea. Other everyday essentials of life, particularly butter and margarine, were becoming increasingly scarce.

It must also be realised that the main method for transporting supplies was horse-drawn so it became necessary for the owners of horses to keep a record of their corn purchases to demonstrate that this commodity was being used efficiently. Another indication of the extent of the shortage of flour is demonstrated by the fact that bakers were offered potatoes to incorporate in their bread-making process. Some bakers stated that they found unspecified substitutes more suitable but the dutiful Mr Pritchard undertook inspections to ensure that any baker making use of potatoes was receiving the correct quantity. In his report recommending the compulsory use of potatoes in bread making, at a ratio of seven units of flour to one unit of potatoes, he praised the efforts of the Fore Street baker, Messrs Hill & Son, who were using potatoes to the fullest extent. With all this additional bureaucracy imposed on local traders one assumes that the Inspector, Mr Pritchard, quickly became one of the least popular men in the town. This view seems to be confirmed by a report he submitted in which he expressed his concern that, having watched a group of soldiers on a route march and eating their lunch, he had noticed that they had left behind the remains of their bread which weighed 3lbs.

Report from Mr Pritchard (Food Inspector) re. wasted bread
(HALS)

(Imperial War Museum)

Several other initiatives were introduced at around this time when the war was about to enter into its fourth year. These included the setting up of a War Distress Fund for the support of local families of men away on service and a War Saving Association and Food Savings Campaign to assist the war effort and educate residents to "husband resources". In support of this the Parish Magazine included regular articles advising housewives on dress economies and providing patterns for making school outfits including a coat, dress and bloomers. The need to make savings in all aspects of life became the order of the day. This could involve the purchase of Exchequer Bonds and War Savings Certificates, economising on food, particularly meat, and even going to bed earlier to reduce the need for fuel and lighting.

To demonstrate that all sections of the community could contribute to the war effort the Parish Magazine published another article in the autumn of 1917, as part of a national appeal, calling on the children of Hatfield to collect conkers. The appeal requested that the children, on this occasion, gave up playing with their conkers but instead collected them for the use of their country. They were being sought for use in the manufacture of munitions in place of corn, thus enabling half a ton of corn to be released for bread making in exchange for every ton of conkers collected. By the end of the conker season Hatfield's children had collected three tons of conkers which had been sent to Hertford for kilning. Special thanks were conveyed to the Boy Scouts and Girl Guides who had responded so well to the request.

Yet another initiative at about this time, though quite controversial at the outset, was the allocation to Hatfield of some 40 prisoners of war for hire by local farmers in small groups. Despite this source of labour being viewed with suspicion initially it undoubtedly proved to be most useful as the number of prisoners employed in Hatfield rose to over 200. Local prisoners of war were accommodated at the workhouse in Union Lane (now Wellfield Road), Newtown House which in addition was also the Headquarters of Lieutenant Mence, Commandant for the area, Chantry House which housed 45 prisoners of war, and the Church Army Rest, while others were billeted in a labour camp at Marshmoor. There are records which indicate that local employers were given the chance to make use of this source of labour as a note has been found clearly stating that one farmer needed the help of "a dozen men for hoeing mangles (sic)". However, his request stressed that he required "men who have done such work before and not anybody who does not know one end of the hoe from the other".

Note asking for POWs to work at Potterells Farm
(HALS)

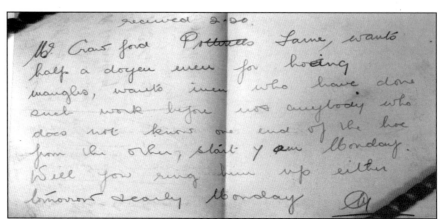

It seems unlikely that the authorities would have paid special attention to the farmer's demands. It is probable that most of the prisoners were employed on the land but at least two of them were assigned to the local Sewage Farm at a rate of 5d (2p) per hour. The District Surveyor, who was responsible for their welfare, successfully applied to the Rural District Council for an extra grant to supply a midday meal to the prisoners which took the form of a loaf of bread for each of them.

There is no evidence to suggest that the employment of prisoners of war caused any serious problems as far as the local residents were concerned but there are reports of attempted escapes during the final weeks of the war. One report in September 1918 appeared under the heading "Hue and Cry throughout Hertfordshire" and related that four POWs had attempted to escape from the camp at Marshmoor and although three of them had been recaptured very quickly one had eluded capture until Sunday when he was found at North Mymms. Then just a few days before the armistice two more prisoners escaped from the same camp and were at liberty for a few days before they were found in a house a couple of miles away, where they had been sheltering and had existed on a diet of local potatoes and turnips which were in plentiful supply. These incidents were probably a small price to pay in view of the contribution they had made in helping to maintain some basic supplies to residents of the district.

Even though the armistice was signed in the first half of November 1918 it must have taken a considerable while before supplies were restored to anything like their normal levels and residents faced another hard winter with shortages still very much in evidence. As Christmas approached Messrs Sherriff, then one of the major local firms responsible for supplying coal throughout the district, warned the Rural District Council that owing to the shortage of coal deliveries they would be unable to provide the service. There is no indication that the Councillors were stirred into action, probably because there was very little that they could do to ease the problem. In fact at the time they appear to have been grappling with the local housing requirements under the "Housing of the Working Classes Reconstruction Scheme". Further evidence that shortages of certain foods continued long after peace was restored is the existence of 'Purchaser's Shopping Cards' for the supply of sugar. The card shows that households had to be registered with a retailer and the weekly allowance was then recorded on the card. In order to minimise the chances of abuse a warning was prominently printed on the card "Penalty for Misuse - £100 Fine or Six Months' Imprisonment or both".

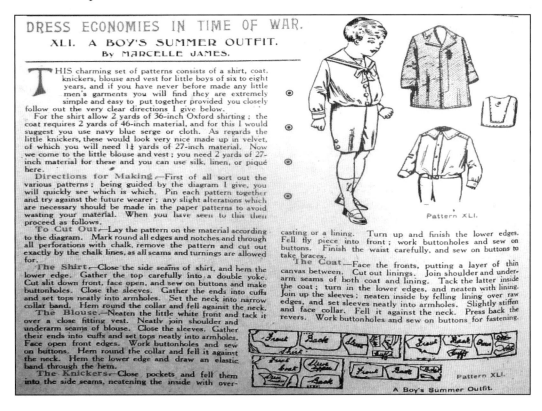

From the Bishops Hatfield Parish Magazine, July 1917

Our Economy Page.

HOW TO MAKE A PRETTY BEST BLOUSE. KITCHEN ECONOMY. GARDEN ECONOMY.

Dress Economy. BY MARCELLE JAMES.

WITH large posters in each district asking us to wear our "Old Clothes in War-time," one feels one cannot go and spend large amounts on the newest blouses which look so very attractive to the eye and pleasing to the mind, but when it is possible to obtain a paper pattern of one of the square-necked blouses for making up at home in an inexpensive material there is no reason why we should not look nicely and neatly dressed, although it is wartime, and money must be saved.

To the man home from mud-stained Flanders or the far flung battle line, there is nothing so refreshing as to see his women folk dainty and neatly dressed.

This charming design needs 2½ yards of 40-inch material. Some of the most charming materials can be bought for about 1s. 6¾d. to 2s. per yard, and if you make the blouse yourself it will cost less than 5s.

Directions for Making.—First of all pin the pattern together and try against the figure. The blouse can be lengthened or shortened as desired at the lower edge, and the sleeve treated in the same way. When you have made any slight alterations that may be necessary, then pin the pattern on the material as shown in diagram. Mark round all edges and notches and through all perforations with tinted chalk. Remove pattern and cut out exactly by the chalk lines, as all seams and turnings are allowed for.

The Making.—Run tucks down side, front pieces and front panel as shown; then join panel in position with beading, being guided by the notches. Close side and shoulder seams with notches matching. French seam the sleeve. Line cuffs, join up and gather sleeve ends into them. Set the tops neatly into armholes, being guided by the notches and binding the raw edges inside with tape. Face open the side edge of blouse, sew on press studs to close, and trim with three small buttons. Turn the neck edges singly down on the right side and those of facings on the wrong side, stitch facing in position. Hem the lower edge of blouse and put a draw string at the back to regulate the fullness round the waist.

If you like you can decorate the neck band with a little hand embroidery, but this you must decide upon for yourself. If you do so, choose an open pattern and work with washing silk.

The pattern of this useful blouse (Pattern XLIV) will be supplied to readers for 4½d. only, post free, on application to the Publishers of HOME WORDS, 11 Ludgate Square, London, E.C.4.

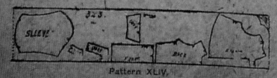

Pattern XLIV.

Kitchen Economy. By Mrs. INCHBOLD.

RICE is often undervalued as a food, though half the people in the world make it their main food, people who work as hard and often harder than the eaters of wheat bread. For the people of India, Japan and China live almost entirely upon rice, and their powers of endurance are second to none. To cook instead of a vegetable, here is an appetizing way. A teacupful of rice in a cloth, not tied up, but folded over to allow room for swelling, in an enamel saucer at bottom of saucepan to pre-

vent the cloth sticking, and then boil till the rice is soft, adding water when necessary to keep the rice covered. When the rice is cooked strain off the water, and here let me advise you to use it instead of starch on your next ironing day. Our grandmothers used rice water starch, and as long as we eat boiled rice with our meals no one need ever be without rice water for starching purposes.

Now put an ounce of good dripping or other fat into a stewpan, melt it, add a finely chopped onion, salt and pepper to taste, and then the rice. Fry all together to a pale fawn colour, moving and turning about to prevent burning. This savoury rice goes well with any kind of meat. With savoury liver or kidney it is economical, as ½ lb. of meat goes far if used in the following way: Cut meat into thin slices, then again into small pieces, and dredge with oatmeal or barley flour. Melt some fat (dripping or margarine) in a stewpan, put in the liver, and cook for five minutes over the fire. Have ready a pint of boiling stock or water, pour over the liver and then simmer until tender. Thicken with a little fine oatmeal, and season with a spoonful of chopped parsley or other favourite herb. When dishing the rice, make a hole in the centre, and then pour in the liver and gravy.

Garden Economy.

By the Rev. F. H. COOKE.

Trenching the Plot.—The sooner you begin this the better for the ground and future crops; it means more frost to kill pests, more air to sweeten the soil, more rain to future plants. Every yard dug before Christmas is worth two dug after that time. Now look at the simple diagram.

X	A			B
	1		3	
	2		4	

A to B represents the surface of the plot. 1 is the first trench of earth. This will be 18 inches in width, 12 in depth. Remove all this soil in 1 to X. Under 1 you have 2. This is what is called subsoil. Do not remove this, but turn it over in the trench, leaving it there. Break it up well. If clayey leave the best part of any soil there is on the *top* of 2. On the top of 2 put in garden refuse and manure. If the ground is very light and sandy do not put in manure till spring. Now turn the soil from trench 3 (which is the same size as trench 1) on to trench 1. Break up trench 4 (which is similar to trench 2) and proceed to the end of the plot when you fill up the last trench with the soil which you took from trench 1 and which you put in a pile called X.

To Store Potatoes.—The majority of small growers will not want to make a "pie." So the crop will be stored in sheds, outhouses and possibly in empty attics. But whatever the place, bear in mind the potato is very soon touched by frost. They should be kept (i) in the dark, (ii) in a cool place, (iii) in a place free from damp, (iv) in a place which is frost-proof. If they are stored in outbuildings use straw, bracken, rough hay or any other good covering material. Let it be put not only on the top, but certainly round the sides. A good covering is worth it when you have laboured for a crop. As you store the potatoes, if possible throw a little fallen lime among them. It should be quite dry when thrown in. It helps to ward off disease.

Carrots, Turnips, Beetroot, Parsnips.—Store as directed above, but using no lime and where possible use any amount of dry sand—except in the case of turnips.

From the Bishops Hatfield Parish Magazine, November 1917

TANK TRIALS IN THE PARK

**The Mark 1 Tank, on display in Hatfield Park,
Between 1919-1969**

In the early weeks of 1916 Hatfield was to be the scene of an important development that was to have a significant effect on the course of the war over the following years. At that time the conflict was well into its second year and thousands of British and Allied troops had been engaged in ferocious battles against the might of the German forces. Losses on both sides had continued to escalate and opposing armies were finding it almost impossible to make real progress as they battled against a determined foe and the mud of Flanders.

With aerial support still in its infancy the British military authorities were anxious to find new ways in which they could gain a significant advantage at the front. Heavier guns were being deployed by both sides but behind the scenes planning was underway in an attempt to produce more sophisticated weapons of war. One of the companies engaged in the planning and development work was Messrs Foster of Lincoln. For some while the firm had been working on a new mobile weapon which, in its early stages, was referred to as a "landship". As developments reached their advanced stages fears were expressed that the use of the word "landship" might leak out and give the enemy a clear indication of what was being planned. In order to maintain a high degree of secrecy the new vehicle should be referred to as a "water carrier". When this proposal reached the "big-wigs" at the Ministry it was immediately rejected as unsuitable and the shorter name of **tank** was proposed and accepted.

It was against this background that Lord Salisbury agreed to the use of land in Hatfield Park for a series of discreet trials of this exciting new weapon. Before the trials began men from the 3rd (Mid Herts) Battalion of the Herts Volunteers Regiment, along with a company of Engineers, lent by the War Office, dug a series of trenches over the planned site. The prototype tank, which was given the name "Mother" but also referred to in correspondence as H M L S Centipede, Big Willie and Little Willie, was transported by train to Hatfield and unloaded by night in preparation for the first trial in the Park on the morning of Saturday 29 January. By 9.15 a.m. an invited audience of approximately 40, comprising mainly members of the armed forces, representatives of Messrs Foster and Lord Salisbury's Agent, Mr McCowen, assembled at the site to witness the initial trials. It was clear that the trial performed well as a second set of trials followed on 2 February. On this occasion the audience was somewhat larger and

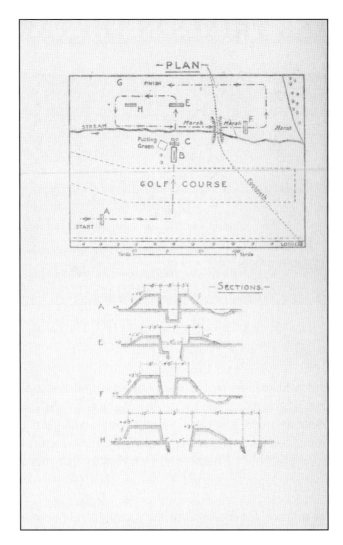

Plan for the Tank Trials in Hatfield Park, 1916

Mother, the original tank.

*(Plan and photograph reproduced from
"Tanks 1914-18. The Log-book of a Pioneer". By Lt. Colonel Sir Albert G. Stern, K.B.E. C.M.G.
Hodder & Stoughton 1919)*

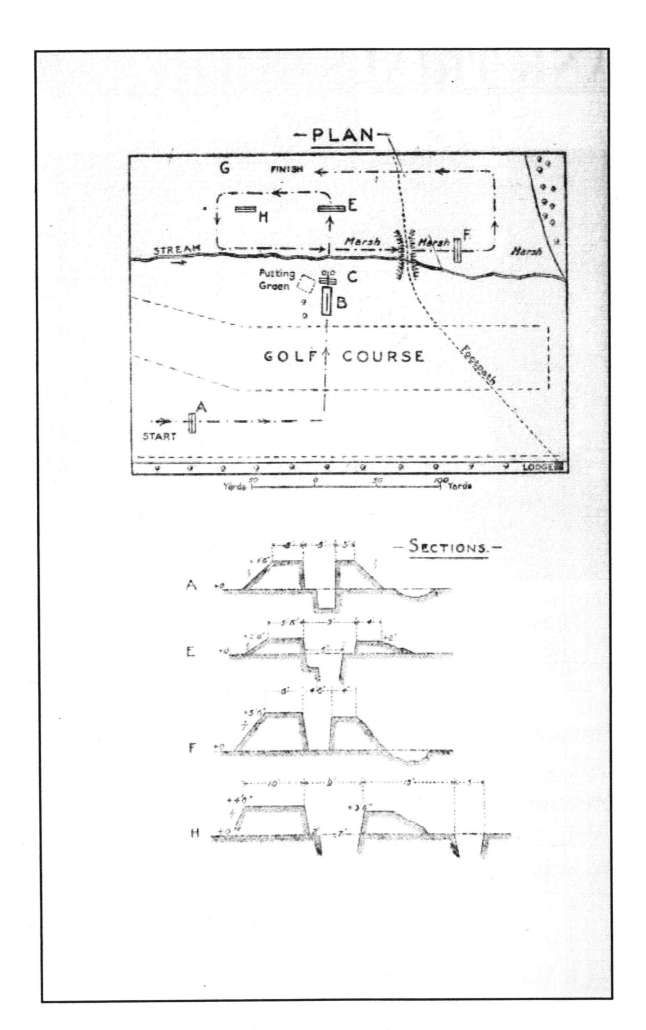

Plan for the Tank Trials in Hatfield Park. 1916

included high-ranking military personnel and leading government ministers.   Those present included Earl Kitchener of Khartoum, David Lloyd George (at that time Minister of Munitions but later that year to become Prime Minister), A J Balfour (former Prime Minister and currently Foreign Secretary), R McKenna (Chancellor of the Exchequer) and many others though it is reported that the Prime Minister, Mr Asquith was unable to attend.   There is no doubt that this elite group of spectators was equally impressed by the performance of the tank as it rumbled over the trial site, across the golf course and perilously close to the putting green, then over a stream and trenches up to nine feet in width, before encountering marshland and other obstacles.

An indication of the excitement that the exercise aroused can be judged by the fact that Mr Balfour, who was a cousin of Lord Salisbury, and therefore was more familiar with the Park than most of the other spectators, decided to take a ride in the tank himself.   However, it was considered that he should not be exposed when it negotiated some of the wider trenches.   Reports state that in order to make his exit he had to be removed from the tank feet first and was heard to express the opinion that there must surely be a more artistic method of leaving a tank.   The Chancellor of the Exchequer, Mr McKenna, endorsed the confidence of the gathering by stating that it was the best investment he had seen and if approved by the military all necessary money would be made available.   For their part, the military representatives shared the enthusiasm for this addition to their armoury and soon began to ask how quickly construction could get underway.

To round off the series of trials, arrangements were made for King George V to visit Hatfield for a demonstration on 8 February and having taken a ride in the tank he expressed the view that it would be a great asset for the army to possess a large number of them.   This provided the seal of approval and gave a considerable boost to the spirits of the country's military and government leaders.   The production line soon began to roll to supply the first of the new tanks in support the troops on the front line.   Records show that 150 of the Mark 1 tanks were built by Messrs Foster and other manufacturers and their successors have developed to become a vital piece of equipment for land-based troops throughout the world ever since.

Tanks were first used in a major battle on 15 September 1916 at the Battle of Flers-Courcelette when 32 Mark 1 were deployed, each with a crew of eight men and a top speed of about 4 m.p.h.   There were two versions of the Mark 1 Tank, described as the male, armed with two six pounder guns and the female with five Vickers Machine Guns.   The Tank Corps was formed in July 1917 and achieved notable successes at the Battle of Cambrai in November 1917 and at Amiens in August 1918.

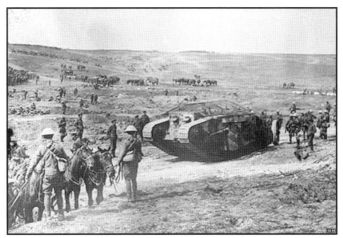

Battle of Flers-Courcelette.
Part of the Franco-British Somme offensive
Summer and Autumn 1916.
(BBC News in Pictures)

In 1919 one of the original Mark 1 tanks was given to the Fourth Marquess to acknowledge Lord Salisbury's cooperation in allowing some of the early tank trials to be held at the Park. The tank was erected on a plinth in the Park, just beyond the viaduct, and became a popular attraction, particularly for children, for the following 50 years. It was eventually donated to the Tank Museum in Bovington. in 1969.

This was not the only piece of armament to find a new home in Hatfield after the war. In May 1919 Lord Salisbury wrote to the Rural District Council to inform them that Hatfield had been offered one of the guns captured by the 4th Bedfordshire Regiment (the old Hartfordshire Militia). It was considered appropriate to recognise those parts of the County where the Battalion had trained by offering the "trophies which it had won". The Council "gratefully accepted" the gift as a tribute of honour to the memory of those who had paid the supreme sacrifice from this neighbourhood in the Great War and by the end of the year confirmed that the gun would be placed on a site near the School House Gardens. There are current residents of Hatfield who recall seeing the gun in later years though the precise location is unclear. It is possible that it was requisitioned for scrap metal during the Second World War, which we understand, almost happened to the tank in the park.

The Gun *(Mill Green Museum)*

GALLANTRY AWARDS & OTHER REWARDS FOR SERVICE

1914/15 Star, British War Medal, Victory Medal

Over many centuries it has become traditional to recognise the invaluable contribution made by those who served the country in its hour of need by the award of campaign and gallantry medals.   The exceptional demands made during the Great War meant that over six million men or their next of kin were entitled to receive some form of recognition for their unprecedented contribution during those years of conflict.

In fact over six and a half million personnel who served were entitled to receive a **British War Medal** and some five and three-quarter million also received a **Victory Medal.**   This latter award bears the dates, 1914-1919 to reflect the extended fighting on some fronts and the signing of the Peace Treaty on 28 June 1919.

Those who served in France and Belgium between the outset of hostilities and 23 November 1914 were entitled to a **1914 Star** (378,000 awarded) and similarly those who served after 23 November 1914 up to the end of 1915 qualified for a **1914-1915 Star** (2,366,000 awarded).

A total of 32 men from the district, listed below, including five who were killed in action, received a range of gallantry decorations.   These included six **Military Crosses (MC) -** distinguished and meritorious service in time of war, seven **Distinguished Conduct Medals (DCM) -** distinguished conduct in the field and sixteen **Military Medals -** bravery in the field.

| MM | DCM | MC |

One man, Private Thomas Alexander Bailiff received the DCM and the MM. Although not originally a Hatfield man, he was working as a gardener in Hatfield Park when war broke out and joined the Hertfordshire Regiment in September1914. There is some confusion as to the date when Thomas was awarded the DCM but it is believed that he won the medal at the battle of Festuberg 18 May 1915, although the London Gazette citation is dated March 11 1916 and reads as follows. –

"Private T A Bailiff, 1st Battalion, Hertfordshire Regiment, T.F. For conspicuous gallantry in rescuing wounded in the open under fire, and continuing his efforts all night until wounded himself."

Also the May 1916, Bishops Hatfield Parish Magazine mentions Thomas's Award for Gallantry –

"Bailiff, Thomas, DCM for saving the life of Lt. the Hon. W. Alexander."

In September 1918 he received the MM.

Pte. Thomas Alexander Bailiff, DCM MM

(This photograph is thought to have been taken after he received the award of the DCM from King George V at Buckingham Palace. Burton Salmon Millennium Exhibition)

The exploits of some of the other men who won these gallantry awards are explained in greater detail elsewhere in this publication. However, special mention should be made of the two men who were decorated by the governments of other Countries. The first of these is Private J. George Harman of the 1st Hertfordshire Regiment who won the Military Medal and the Belgian Croix de Guerre. The second was Lieutenant Basil Blackett who served both in the Australian and British forces. Initially a soldier, he

**Belgian
Croix de Guerre**

**French
Croix de Guerre**

Legion d'Honneur

achieved the rank of corporal then trained as an observer and air gunner. He was commissioned and seconded to the Royal Flying Corps and then to the Royal Air Force before becoming a full member of the RAF. He was credited with five aerial victories and was awarded the Belgian Croix de Guerre, the French Croix de Guerre and the Legion d'Honneur. Basil Blackett spent his early life living with his family at St Michael's, a substantial property at Woodside, Hatfield and attended Eton College.

It should also be mentioned that when medals were sent to next of kin following the death of the recipient two other items were also sent: firstly, a large, bronze **Memorial Plaque**, bearing the words, *He Died For Freedom And Honour*, (sometimes referred to as 'A Dead Man's Penny') and secondly, a scroll bearing the name, rank and regiment of the individual concerned.

Finally, one other item was issued to those who were honourably discharged as a result of their wounds or sickness. This was the **Silver War Badge**, which came into being in 1916, following the introduction of conscription. It carried the wording, *For King and Empire Services Rendered* in recognition of those who served and thus it distinguished them from those who never joined up.

Bronze Memorial Plaque

Silver War Badge

The town of Hatfield also decided to issue its own *In Memoriam and Roll of Honour Album* to commemorate the "Signing of Peace and as a token of Grateful Remembrance". The Album lists the names and regiments of over 800 men from the district, who served in the forces during the war years, including 141 who lost their lives. Every returning serviceman had the opportunity to have a copy of the Album, with his name inscribed on the front cover, or alternatively could choose to have a commemorative silver matchbox. For those who did not return their next of kin was offered the same choice. (See also - Armistice and Peace Celebrations.)

Hatfield Men Gallantry Awards

Private	Thomas	Bailiff	DCM, MM	1st Herts Regiment
Lieutenant	Basil	Blackett	BCdG, FCdG, LdH	RAF
Major	William	Bond	DCM	Essex Regiment
Sergeant Major	F.	Brown	MM	Royal Engineers
Captain	F.C.	Burgess	MC	Royal Field Artillery
Leading Stoker	F.G.	Castle	DSM	Royal Navy
Captain	J.A.	Cecil	MC	Royal Field Artillery. KIA
Major	Geoffrey	Church	MC	Royal Field Artillery
Staff Sergeant Major	A.E.	Cousins	MSM	Royal Army Service Corps
Private	John	Currell	MM	1st West Yorks Regiment. KIA
Sergeant	Leonard	Easton	MM	1st Herts Regiment
Sergeant	Arthur	Freeman	MM	Royal Garrison Artillery
Private	William	Groom	MM	1st Herts Regiment
Private	George	Harman	MM	1st Herts Regiment
Sergeant	Ireton	Hickson	MM	1st Herts Regiment
Sergeant	George	Ling	MM	1st Herts Regiment
Lt. Colonel	Frederick	Lloyd	CM, CBE	Royal Ordinances
Captain	Cecil	O'Bury	MC	1st Herts Regiment
Sergeant	Stephen	Osborn	DCM	1st Herts Regiment. KIA
Private	Alexander	Page	MM	1st Herts Regiment
Sergeant	Harry	Randall	DCM	1st Herts Regiment. KIA
Private	F.R.	Reynolds	MM	Royal Army Service Corps
Private	Robert	Sear	MM	Beds Regiment
Sergeant	G.T.	Sharp	DCM, MM	Grenadier Guards
Captain	Harold	Sheehan	MC	Royal Irish Rifles
Captain	Leslie	Smith	MC	8th London Regiment
Sergeant	Henry	Stallon	DCM	7th Beds Regiment
Private	Willam	Stevens	MM	East Surrey Regiment
Corporal	Percy	Taylor	MM	Royal Engineers
Sergeant	Sidney	Walby	MM	2nd Beds Regiment. KIA
Sergeant	L.	Wren	MM	1st Herts Regiment

MC	Military Cross
DCM	Distinguished Conduct Medal
DSM	Distinguished Service Medal
MM	Military Medal
CM	Companion of St. Michael and St. George
CBE	Commander of the British Empire
LdH	Legion d' Honneur
BCdG	Belgian Croix de Guerre
FCdG	French Croix de Guerre

ARMISTICE & PEACE CELEBRATIONS IN HATFIELD

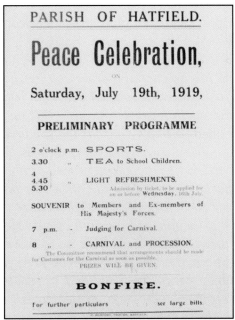

Celebration Poster
(HALS)

The local press proudly reported events in the following glowing terms:-

"The glad news of the end of hostilities became known in Hatfield about midday on Monday (11 November) and although there was no great outburst of feeling flags sprang up in every direction and youngsters soon began perambulating the streets cheering, singing and waving their union jacks. A well-attended meeting was held at St. Audrey's, at which the Rector (the Rev. J J Antrobus) presided and arrangements were made for the holding of an open-air thanksgiving service on the following day. On Tuesday there was a special celebration of Holy Communion at the parish church, attended by a very large number of communicants. The munitions works of Messrs Waters & Sons were closed for the day, the tradesmen closed their shops at midday for some hours and farmers and other employers of labour allowed their work people time off. Shortly before one o'clock crowds began to assemble in the square and were quickly marshalled under the direction of Mr P R Bassett. At one o'clock the procession began to move off. First came the churchwardens and sexton each carrying his staff of office, the choir of the parish church, the organist and the Rev J B Hunt in surplices. Then followed in order the uniformed nurses from the VAD hospital with several wounded soldiers. Discharged soldiers and sailors, Hatfield Fire Brigade, Cadet Corps, Boy Scouts, Girl Guides, women workers (needlework), forestry girls, women workers on the land, munitions workers in their working attire, railwaymen, members of the Foresters' Court and Oddfellows' Lodge, children with flags and special constables".

"The procession was flanked by crowds of townsfolk and large numbers from the out-lying districts, and with due solemnity and decorum moved up Fore Street, past the parish church where the bells were ringing out such a joyous peel as had not been heard for more than four years, and lined up in the great quadrangle at Hatfield House".

"On the steps of the ancestral home of the Cecil family the clergy and choir took up their stand and the service commenced with the singing of the grand old hymn 'All people that on earth do dwell'. Then followed the Lord's Prayer, and never perhaps in Hatfield before was that simple prayer voiced with more heartfelt fervour. The Rector read a prayer for all monarchs, presidents and rulers and then followed that beautiful prayer for our sailors and soldiers 'O Almighty Lord God, we commend to your fatherly goodness', so oft repeated in our churches and schools during the years of war. Prayer for the

departed was followed by the singing of the hymn 'O God, our help in ages past'. A few clearly-spoken simple but correct words from the Rector, words that will be ever-remembered".

It seems worthwhile quoting the words of the Rector as they serve to capture the mood of the nation, the sense of relief and the euphoria that prevailed after more than four years of unimaginable strife.

" Men, women and children this is the day which we have waited four and a quarter years for, longed for, prayed for, and now that it has come it is so sacred that we can hardly realise the greatness of it all. In the days to come your children will ask you what you did and what it felt like when Britain and her allies came out of the greatest war that the world has ever known. Tell them that the first thing the people of Great Britain did was to gather together to thank God for the great victory. Parliament went forthwith to St. Margaret's to return thanks for the crowning victory, crowds made their way to the palace of the King who had led them so simply and yet so steadfastly through the dark days. Tell them about this place, how they all gathered together and poured up the old street past the church while the bells from the old tower rang out as they never rang for years. Tell them of the men in blue and the women of Hatfield who had nursed them back to health and strength again, of the women on the land and in the woods who had toiled for their country because there were no men, of the men who had fought and were unable to fight longer, the women who had given every afternoon to care for the sick and wounded, and all who had taken any part in helping towards a great end. Tell them they were all there to render thanks for the glorious victory. Tell them there was enough to eat in those days but nothing more – enough to eat because the great British Navy held its grip. Tell them of our glorious sailors and soldiers who were loyal to the death. Tell them in the years to come of the thankfulness to God, Who has given us a great victory."

After a moment's silent pause the Rector added "In honour of the Navy I ask you now to sing '*Rule Britannia'*." The first verse was then sung and afterwards the three verses of the National Anthem.

The report goes on to sum up the occasion by explaining that after this simple but dignified, earnest service had been concluded, one of the greatest, if not the greatest local gatherings that had ever assembled in front of the historic mansion quietly dispersed to take up again the 'trivial round, the common task'. Meanwhile frantic efforts were made on Tuesday to get as many as possible of the street lamps in working order after more than three and a half years, and the lights at night brought people out in large numbers. Barrels of tar were brought to the square and while an indulgent police officer was looking the other way someone applied a light and the deafening cheers rose as an effigy of the ex-Kaiser was carried round and committed to the flames. A bugle band headed a procession of munitions girls that paraded the chief thoroughfares singing patriotic songs and waving union jacks.

Undoubtedly the armistice brought with it a tremendous feeling of relief for the whole population after four years of unimaginable suffering but the expressions of joy and the celebrations that the announcement provoked must have been dimmed by the sadness of the losses that had affected the lives of so many families. Life could begin to get back to something like normality for the bulk of the population as they welcomed home the men who had served their country in its hour of need but the world would never be quite the same after the horrors that had been experienced. Furthermore, whilst the fighting at the front had come to an end it was several months before peace was formally restored. Discussions on the terms of the peace treaty soon got under way, involving the leaders of Britain, France, Italy and the USA but it was not until 28 June 1919 that all parties sat down to sign to sign the Treaty of Versailles.

Whilst the nation had been immensely relieved to know that the fighting had come to an end they knew that peace would not be fully restored until the treaty had been signed. Communities throughout the country had spent the early months of 1919 awaiting the final announcement and were vigorously making preparations for the celebrations that would take place in every town and village once their leaders had reached their final agreement. The townsfolk of Hatfield were keen and ready for this occasion and Saturday 19 July 1919 was the chosen day to mark this happy event throughout the whole country. A Public Meeting was arranged at the Public Hall to discuss the arrangements on Thursday, 3 July and some 200 residents attended the meeting.

(HALS)

List of Sports Events
(*HALS*)

It was decided that in addition to the celebrations a Thanksgiving Service would be held at 3.00 pm on Sunday 3 August and Lady Salisbury had already proposed that she would entertain all those who had served with the Forces accompanied by two friends each on the following Tuesday. It was agreed that the main celebration would take the form of a carnival and a committee was formed from all sections of the community, including six former servicemen, to make the necessary arrangements.

The atmosphere that prevailed throughout the town can be best captured by quoting from the press reports of the day as reported by the Herts Advertiser under the headline *'High Jinks at Hatfield'*.

"Great rejoicing prevailed at Hatfield on Saturday as 'The Day' so long awaited had come. The town was prettily decorated Fore Street and Park Street being a mass of flags. During the afternoon athletic sports took place in Hatfield Park. The Sports Committee had made very able preparations so that the events quickly followed one another. The handicappers who officiated were W R Watson, who, incidentally, had spent the final months of the conflict as a prisoner of war, E J Scott and J Andrews. The races were started by Messrs Gow, Ellingham and R E Whitby while Messrs Dickinson, Sharpe, Kekewich, S Hankin, F Richardson, Owers and J Walby were at the tape to pick out the winners.

Many of the races created great excitement as they were won by inches only. Much amusement was caused in the many competitions such as, the boot race, 4 legged race, boat race, tilting the bucket, wrestling (pick a-back) and greasy pole. In the last event the undaunted spirit of the Land Girls was much in evidence. The Marathon Race, run over almost 3 miles, was won comfortably by A Wiltshire while Ed

Hickson won the high jump at 5ft 1in. narrowly beating his brother, Ernest Hickson. There were also sports held for the school children. These were keenly contested, some fine sprinting being shown."

"When they were over the children had a 'bumper' tea and were kindly looked after by their teachers and friends. A delightful programme of music was given by a band supplied by Messrs Ashton & Mitchell's Music Agency, London. During the afternoon tea was provided in the Old Palace and there was no cause for complaint. At 7.30 the prizes which were numerous and costly were presented to the successful competitors by Lady Salisbury."

PEACE CELEBRATIONS.
HATFIELD.

Prizes for Sports.

Open only to Demobilised Sailors, Soldiers, and Airmen.

			£. s. d.
One Mile Race	3 Prizes		4 : 0 : 0
Half Mile.	3 "		2 : 10 : 0
Quarter Mile	3 "		2 : 10 : 0
100 Yards.	3 "		2 : 0 : 0
Relay.	4 "		2 : 0 : 0

Open to Residents of Hatfield Parish.

Marathon Race	3 Prizes		6 : 0 : 0
High Jump	2 "		2 : 0 : 0
Long Jump	2 "		2 : 0 : 0
Boat Race	7 "	3/-	1 : 1 : 0
Tug-of-War	8 "	4/-	1 : 12 : 0
Sack Race	2		1 : 0 : 0
Boot Race	2 "		1 : 0 : 0
Bolster Spar	2 "		1 : 0 : 0
Tilting the Bucket	4 "		1 : 0 : 0
Thread-the-Needle Race	4 "		1 : 0 : 0
Hurdle Race	2 "		2 : 0 : 0
Four-legged Race	6		1 : 0 : 0
Obstacle Race	2 "		2 : 0 : 0
Wrestle, (Pick-a-back)	4 "		1 : 0 : 0
Veterans Race	2 "		1 : 0 : 0
Climb the Pole, for a Leg of Mutton.			
Skipping, Ladies any age, (Race)	2 Prizes		1 : 0 : 0

Total £38 13 0

List of Prizes
(*HALS*)

57

BY APPOINTMENT

TELEGRAMS:
"ORAMA, PICCY, LONDON."

TELEPHONE:
7981 GERRARD. (5 LINES.)
4040 MAYFAIR. (2 LINES.)

ASHTON & MITCHELL'S ROYAL AGENCY
(ASHTON & MITCHELL LTD)
33, OLD BOND STREET,

LONDON, W.1.

14th July 1919.

J.Taylor Whincatt Esq,
Messrs. Pryor Reid & Co.Ltd.
The Brewery. Hatfield.

Dear Sir,

We beg to confirm having engaged our Band of 10
performers to play at your Sports at Hatfield on Saturday
next, Peace Day, for a fee of 35 guineas, plus rail fares
(third class)

The musicians will leave Kings Cross by the 1-10
arriving Hatfield 1-41 where we understand you will very
kindly have them met with a conveyance. It is with much
regret we must ask you to let them return on the 6-17 as
some of the men are playing elsewhere in the evening, but
we feel sure you will to some extent appreciate the difficulties
of this particular day.

Will you very kindly have a <u>Piano</u> available for their
use, this is very important as we are anxious to get as much
volume as we possibly can, also if it is possible to arrange
a few wooden boards to form a platform for them to play on it
would increase the sound.

Mr. Haxton will be in charge of the Band, which
we feel sure will give you satisfaction.

We are, Sir,
Yours faithfully,
ASHTON & MITCHELL Ltd.

Director.

Hiring the Band
(*HALS*)

"While this was taking place a very large number of people in fancy dress had assembled on the north front of Hatfield House. The costumes were exceptionally fine and considering the very numerous entries judging the prize winners was no easy matter. The task was ably carried out by Mrs McCowen, Miss Blackett, Rev. J B Hunt and Mr F W Speaight who no doubt gave entire satisfaction.

A procession round the town was afterwards started. There were costumed boys and girls, ladies and gentlemen; decorated baby cars and cycles while in the rear emblematic vehicles were to be seen. There were exceptionally pretty 'Britannia', 'The Fairy Glen' and 'The Forest Girls' which looked charming and 'The Trial of the Kaiser' with his final hanging caused much mirth. On the procession arriving back at the House the successful competitors received their prizes from the hands of Lady Salisbury, each winner applauded by the dense throng. Prize winners included 'Mad Hatter', 'The People', 'Eastern Maiden', 'Dick Whittington', 'Early Victorian Crinoline', 'Result of High Prices', Wanted a Horse', 'Peace Cycle', 'Windmill', 'Nigger Bridal Pair', 'Village Gossip', 'Tramp', 'Lost Spirit', 'Britannia' 'Fairy Glen' and 'Forest Girls'.

A few minutes had elapsed when a huge 'bang' was heard. Not an air raid alarm but a prelude to the firework display. Despite the rain many people stayed to watch the gorgeous display after which a bonfire was lit. This burnt beautifully, a sight which all will remember for years to come.

The excellent way in which all the secretarial duties had been so efficiently carried out so that everything went well reflects to the great credit on Messrs E J Dunham and A W Whitby."

As already mentioned in the "Gallantry Awards & Other Rewards for Service" chapter the Peace Celebrations Committee decided to issue an "In Memoriam and Roll of Honour Album" or a Silver Matchbox which was paid for by the Hatfield Parish Council. This seemed to be a straightforward choice in recognition of the community's gratitude towards all those who had served in the armed forces and as such would be welcomed by the recipients. However correspondence has come to light that shows that even when they presented with a perfectly simple choice you can't please all the people all the time! In a letter to the committee, Lance Corporal C. M. Panter, writing on behalf of some of his colleagues, sought more details of the silver matchbox before making their choice. Apparently they had been sent a very full description of the Album that was being offered but very little about the style of the matchbox. The request for information was immediately rejected and the men, therefore, had to make their choice on the information already made available. Lance Corporal Panter, in late 1917, was Company Sergeant Major of No.4. (Hatfield) Company, 3rd Battalion the Hertfordshire Regiment. He was later called up and served with the Essex Regiment as a Lance Corporal.

The Silver Matchbox

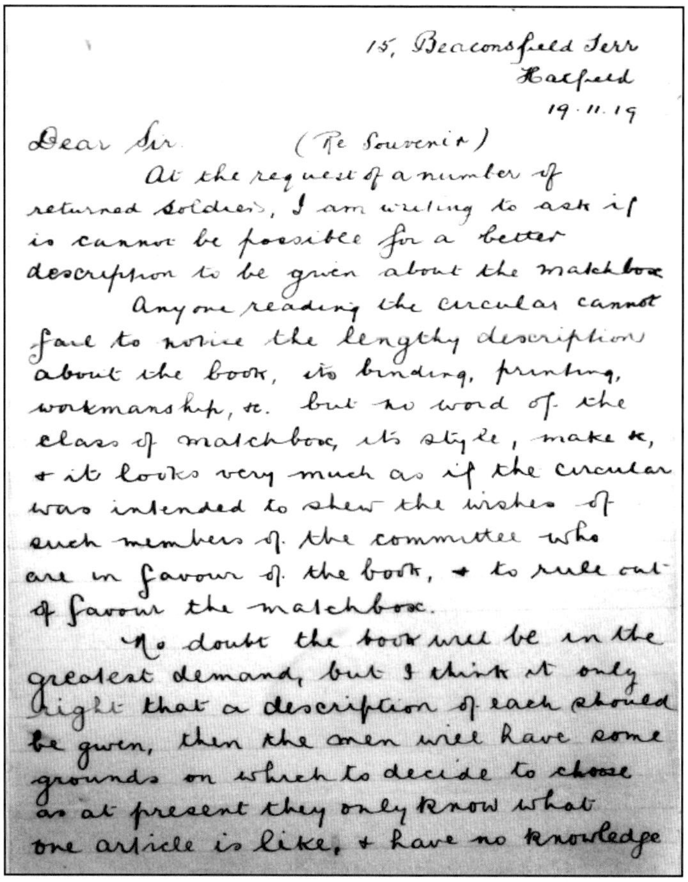

15, Beaconsfield Terr
Hatfield
19·11·19

Dear Sir,   (Re Souvenir)

At the request of a number of returned soldiers, I am writing to ask if is cannot be possible for a better description to be given about the matchbox

Any one reading the circular cannot fail to notice the lengthy description about the book, its binding, printing, workmanship, &c. but no word of the class of matchbox, its style, make &c, & it looks very much as if the circular was intended to shew the wishes of such members of the committee who are in favour of the book, & to rule out of favour the matchbox.

No doubt the book will be in the greatest demand, but I think it only right that a description of each should be given, then the men will have some grounds on which to decide to choose as at present they only know what one article is like, & have no knowledge at all of what the box is like

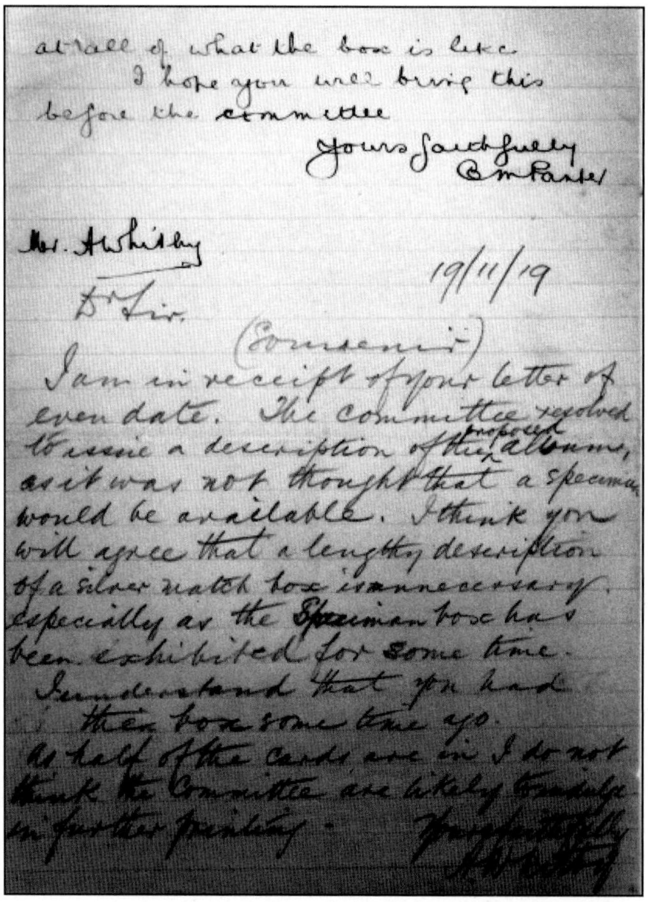

I hope you will bring this before the committee

Yours faithfully
C M Panter

Mr. A Whitby
                    19/11/19

D Sir
            (Souvenir)
I am in receipt of your letter of even date. The committee resolved to issue a description of the Album, as it was not thought that a Specimen would be available. I think you will agree that a lengthy description of a silver match box is unnecessary, especially as the Specimen box has been exhibited for some time. I understand that you had the box some time ago. As half of the cards are in I do not think the Committee are likely to indulge in further printing.

Yours faithfully
A Whitby

Letter from Lance Corporal C. M. Panter
(HALS)

It should be explained that there are several differences when comparing the names of those listed on the War Memorial and those in the In Memoriam section of the Album. In view of this 172 names of servicemen who lost their lives have been researched whilst undertaking this project and this has resulted in 2 additional names being added to the Hatfield War Memorial, Private Percy Frederick Bean and Private Henry W. Bishop. It is impossible to provide a full explanation for all the variations that exist between the names on the War Memorial and those in the Album except to say that the lists were drawn up by two different committees who set different criteria. Whilst many of the men came from well-established local families there are a number whose links with the Hatfield district were rather more tenuous. It should also be made clear that several of the names on the Hatfield War Memorial appear on village memorials.

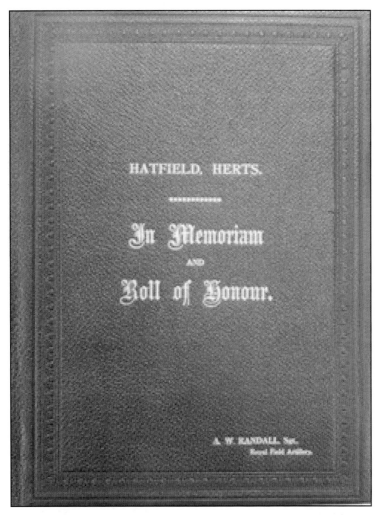

The "In Memoriam & Roll of Honour" Album

An interesting insight into the deliberations that took place when deciding on names to be included is provided in a letter (see below), sent to the committee by a local resident, Mr Tweedie of Ludwick Corner, Hatfield. In his letter he brings to their attention the role of his daughter, Christian Forbes Guest, née Tweedie, who had worked as a nurse both in the French Military Nursing Service and in a British Military Hospital throughout the war. Her service included a spell at Le Havre Hospital from the beginning of 1915 and subsequently at the Hatfield VAD Hospital. He also referred to another young woman Annie Bain (?) who similarly had worked in a VAD Military Hospital in France for about two years *"under heavy bombing and machine gun fire on various occasions"*. Therefore, he felt that there was a strong case for these two women to be included in the Roll of Honour section of the album. The committee viewed it very differently, ruling that those listed should be limited to ex-servicemen and those who remained in one of the services. Such decisions illustrate the prevailing attitude to women despite the unprecedented demands that had been made on them over the war years.

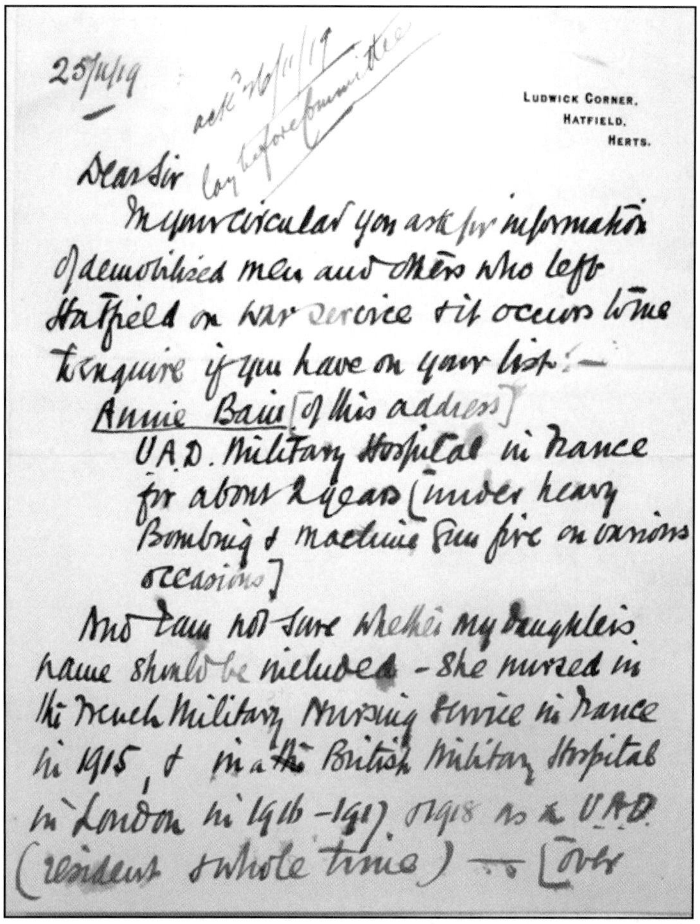

25/11/19

ackd 26/11/19

Lay before Committee

Ludwick Corner,
Hatfield,
Herts.

Dear Sir

In your circular you ask for information of demobilised men and others who left Hatfield on war service & it occurs to me to enquire if you have on your list:—

Annie Bain [of this address]

V.A.D. Military Hospital in France for about 2 years [under heavy Bombing & machine Gun fire on various occasions]

And I am not sure whether my daughter's name should be included – she nursed in the French Military Nursing Service in France in 1915, & in the British Military Hospital in London in 1916–1917 & 1918 as a V.A.D. (resident & whole time) – Over

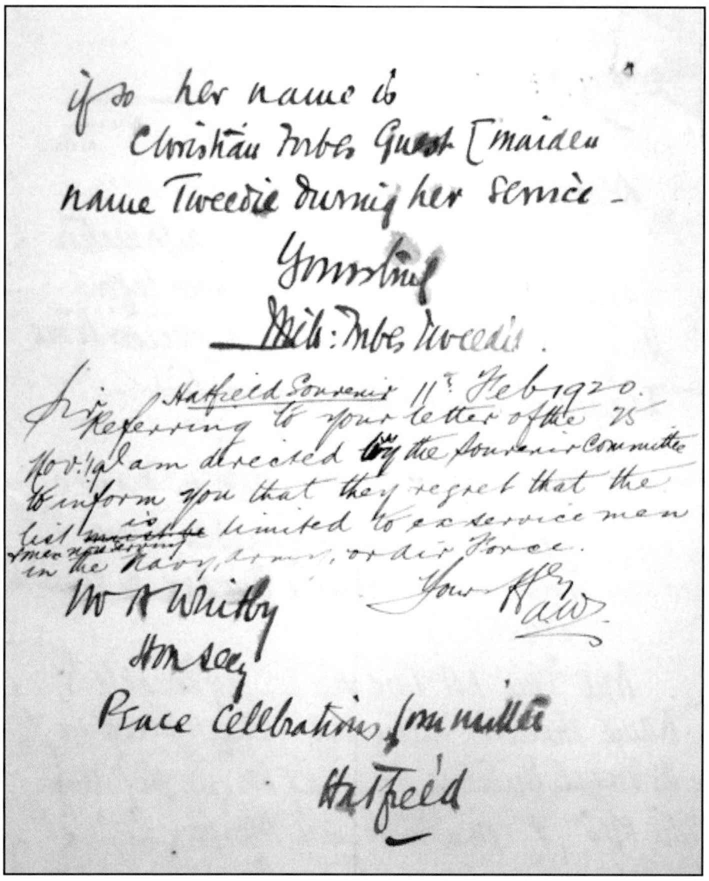

if so her name is

Christian Forbes Guest [maiden name Tweedie during her service –

Yours truly

Wili: Forbes Tweedie.

Sir, Hatfield Souvenir 11th Feb 1920.

Referring to your letter of the 25 Nov: 19 I am directed by the Souvenir Committee to inform you that they regret that the list ~~must be~~ is limited to ex service men & men who served in the Navy, Army, or Air Force.

Yours [illegible]

Mr H Whitby

Hon Secy

Peace Celebrations Committee

Hatfield

Letter from Mr Tweedie of Ludwick Corner

(HALS)

HATFIELD'S WAR MEMORIALS

Hatfield War Memorial

By the end of 1918 the survivors of the conflict were returning to their homes, seeking to adjust to civilian life in a changed world and the nation's thoughts were beginning to turn to ways in which the supreme sacrifice that had been made by so many of their relations and colleagues could be commemorated.

On 19 December Lord Salisbury chaired a meeting held in the Public Hall to discuss the form that the town's war memorial should take. A wide range of suggestions poured forth both in terms of its form and its location. A cottage hospital was proposed as was an institute "for amusement and instruction of the inhabitants of Hatfield" and as regards its location the alternatives were equally diverse. The Rector suggested a site in the Churchyard whilst others, including Dr. Lovell Drage, suggested that it should be close to where some of the fallen townsfolk were buried in the churchyard at St Luke's Church in St Albans Road. Having listened to the numerous views expressed it was concluded that the matter should be progressed in a traditional British manner by the formation of a committee.

This did not prove to be a delaying tactic as the Committee set about its task and within a few weeks had rejected suggestions that it should take the form of a hospital, an institute and baths. It was their firm view that it should be a 'pure memorial' to perpetuate the memory of those who had died and be a reminder for all time. The siting of the proposed memorial was then discussed and four possible locations emerged. Two of these were at the entrance to or in the Parish Churchyard; another was alongside the Park Gates, opposite the station and a fourth site suggested was at the Ryde Field. Now, a century later, it is interesting to observe that had this fourth site been chosen the memorial would have stood precisely where the re-aligned Hertford Road now meets the Great North Road. Thus, it would have created an additional problem for the town planners when this area was developed some forty years later.

Hatfield War Memorial

COMMITTEE.

The Marquess of Salisbury, K.G., G.C.V.O., C.B.
Lady Gwendolen Cecil.
Sir William Church, Bart., K.C.B.
Rev. J. J. Antrobus, M.A.
Mr. V. Austin.
Mr. T. W. M. Bennett.
Mr. Birch.
Rev. W. Buzza.
Mr. D. Crawford.
Mr. J. R. Sheehan-Dare.
Mr. H. Ewington.
Mr. J. Gregory.
Mr. J. Halsey.
Mr. Ivory.
Lieut.-Col. W. J. Halsey.
Miss Kendall.
Mr. H. Lawrence.
Mr. J. Lloyd.
Mr. Massam.
Mr. Oliver.
Mr. Page.
Mr. W. J. Phillips.
Mr. A. W. Reeks.
Mr. W. J. Richardson.
Mr. F. W. Speaight.
Mr. E. T. Tingey.
Mr. T. G. Walker.
Mr. Willes.

Mr. E. J. PRITCHARD, *Hon. Secretary,*
Bunnyfield House, Hatfield.

Mr. BROUGH GIRLING
(Messrs. Barclay's Bank), *Hon. Treasurer.*

Having arrived at this point the Committee felt that, rather than make an instant decision, a sub-committee should be formed with a brief to find an architect who would recommend not only the most appropriate possible site, but also provide an estimate of the cost. The sub-committee acted positively and by the end of March Mr H. Baker, one of the most eminent architects in England who had been responsible for government buildings in Pretoria and Delhi, had been selected to undertake the work. He had visited Hatfield and it was decided that his strong recommendation, in favour of the site alongside the Park Gates, should be accepted. The estimated cost was to be in the region of £1500.

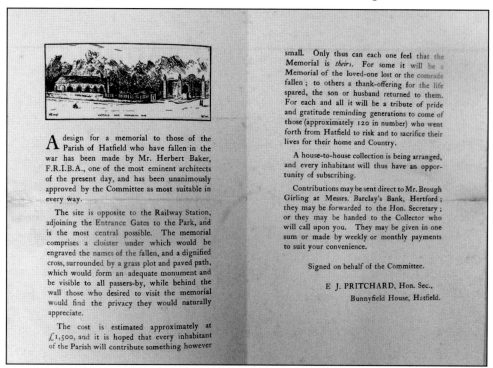

A design for a memorial to those of the Parish of Hatfield who have fallen in the war has been made by Mr. Herbert Baker, F.R.I.B.A., one of the most eminent architects of the present day, and has been unanimously approved by the Committee as most suitable in every way.

The site is opposite to the Railway Station, adjoining the Entrance Gates to the Park, and is the most central possible. The memorial comprises a cloister under which would be engraved the names of the fallen, and a dignified cross, surrounded by a grass plot and paved path, which would form an adequate monument and be visible to all passers-by, while behind the wall those who desired to visit the memorial would find the privacy they would naturally appreciate.

The cost is estimated approximately at £1,500, and it is hoped that every inhabitant of the Parish will contribute something however small. Only thus can each one feel that the Memorial is *theirs*. For some it will be a Memorial of the loved-one lost or the comrade fallen ; to others a thank-offering for the life spared, the son or husband returned to them. For each and all it will be a tribute of pride and gratitude reminding generations to come of those (approximately 120 in number) who went forth from Hatfield to risk and to sacrifice their lives for their home and Country.

A house-to-house collection is being arranged, and every inhabitant will thus have an opportunity of subscribing.

Contributions may be sent direct to Mr. Brough Girling at Messrs. Barclay's Bank, Hertford ; they may be forwarded to the Hon. Secretary ; or they may be handed to the Collector who will call upon you. They may be given in one sum or made by weekly or monthly payments to suit your convenience.

Signed on behalf of the Committee.

E J. PRITCHARD, Hon. Sec.,
Bunnyfield House, Hatfield.

When the decision to proceed was announce the Rector, the Rev. J. J. Antrobus, referred to the amount of money that Hatfield ought to be able to raise and without wishing to dictate the sum that should be given, he urged the public to remember that anything they could give would be as nothing compared with that which had been given by those whose memory they wished to perpetuate. The hope was expressed that some contribution, however small, would be made by every inhabitant of the parish. A further appeal was made to local residents to ensure that they provided details of all those men whose details should appear on the memorial.

Whilst a prompt decision was made on the form and location of the town's war memorial erection of the building and its surrounding garden took somewhat longer to complete and a further two years elapsed before the War Memorial was dedicated. It was on the afternoon of Sunday 12 June 1921 that a large crowd assembled along the Great North Road despite threatening rain to witness the ceremony of dedication.

Invitations to the enclosure of the memorial garden had to be restricted to immediate relations of those who were commemorated and the large body of ex-servicemen from the parish. A procession consisting of the Band, Choir, Bishop of Exeter and Clergy proceeded from the Public Hall to be joined at the park gates by the Lord Lieutenant, Lord Hampden, Lord Salisbury, Sir Hildred Carlile and Colonel Halsey. The service opened with the singing of "For all the Saints". Before unveiling the memorial Lord Hampden gave an eloquent speech in which he reminded those present that they were gathered there on the anniversary of the Battle of Ypres, where so many of the men from the neighbourhood gave their lives. The Bishop of Exeter then dedicated the Cross and was followed by Lord Salisbury who read the Roll of Honour. After the Last Post and Reveille were sounded, relations of the men from the parish commemorated on the memorial came forward to lay their wreaths at the foot of the Cross. The whole ceremony must have been a very moving occasion for all who had gathered there on that June afternoon, but for none more so than for the Bishop of Exeter, Lord William Cecil, the younger brother of the 4th Marquess of Salisbury.   This memorial, set in a peaceful garden, by the gates to Hatfield Park on the Great North Road, stands as a lasting tribute from the people of Hatfield to the local men who made the supreme sacrifice for their country.

Hatfield Memorial Dedication Ceremony
Sunday 12 June 1921
(Hatfield Library)

Hatfield Memorial and Gardens

Hatfield War Memorial Names

Adams, E.W. Pte. 1st Herts Regt.
Andrews, W. J. Pte. Beds Regt. 1st Bn.
Angell, F. T. Pte. 6th Royal Berks Regt.
Austin, C. J. Sgt. Northumberland Fus.
Austin, C. J. 2nd Lt. K.O.R Lancs Regt.
Austin, V. J. Pte. London Rifle Brig.
Baker, A. A. Pte. Canadian Seaforth Highlanders
Baker, H. J. Pte. Northamptonshire Regt.
Basil, F. Pte. 1st Herts Regt.
Beach, H. Pte. 1st East Kent Regt.
Bean, F.P. Pte. North Lancs Regt.
Berry, W. H. Pte. 6th Beds Regt.
Birch, S. Pte. 8th Royal Fusiliers
Bishop, H.W. Pte. Duke of Cornwall's Light Inf.
Bray, C.W. Gunner, Herts Royal Field Artillery
Bray, H. W. Corp. Herts Regt.
Buck, W. Gunner, Royal Field Artillery
Butterworth, A. Pte. Royal Army Service Corps.
Caesar, P. Lt. 7th Shropshire Light Infantry
Canham, J. H. Pte. 1st Herts. Regt.
Cecil, G. E. 2nd Lt. Grenadier Guards
Cecil, J. A. Gascoyne (MC) Capt. Royal Field Artillery.
Cecil. R. W. Gascoyne Lt. Royal Horse Artillery
Cecil, R. E. Gascoyne Lieut. 4th Beds. Regt.
Chandler, C. Sgt. 2nd Beds Regt.
Church, J. W. Capt. 1st Herts Regt.
Coe, J. J. Lance-Corp. 1st Herts Regt.
Cooper, F. C. Pte. 1st Herts Regt.
Cooper, G. E. L-Corp. 23rd Middx Regt.
Cooper, W. J. Pte. 8th Beds. Regt.
Currell, G. A. Pte. Notts. & Derbyshire Regt.
Currell, J. T. (MM) Pte. 1st West Yorks. Regt.
Davies, W. G. Pte. 24th Canadians
Davies, H. Q-M Sgt. Machine Gun Corps.
Dodds, T. G. Pte. Royal Army Service Corps
Dollemore, A. J. A. Pte. Royal West Kent Regt.
Drummond, M. Pte. London Scottish Regt.
Fox, W. H. Pte. 1st/5th Beds Regt.
Freeman, H. E. Pte. 7th Beds Regt.
Frost, J. Pte. Royal Army Service Corps.
Frost, J. C. Pte. 1st Herts Regt.
Garland, C. H. Pte. Royal Army Service Corps.

Gentle, L. J. Sapper, Royal Engineers
Gittings, J. W. L-Corp. Herts Regt.
Goodman, W. M. Pte. Suffolk Reg.
Goody, G. R. Lt. K. O. R. Rifle Corps.
Goody, G. A. 2nd Lt. K. O. R. Rifle Corps.
Green, J. E. Sapper, Royal Engineers
Greenham, F. H. J. Sapper, Royal Eng.
Gregory, H. Pte. 1st Hon. Artillery Comp.
Griffin, T. G. Pte. Pte. 4th Beds Regt.
Groom, D. Pte. 5th Royal Irish Fusiliers
Hall, H. J. Pte. 1st Herts Regt.
Hall, R. W. Pte. 1st Herts Regt.
Halsey, A. E. Pte. 1st Lincs Regt.
Halsey, F. G. Pte. 14th Northumberland Fusiliers
Hawthorne, E. F. Trooper, Household Battalion.
Hedger, J. Pte. 7th Beds Regt.
Hill, W. A. Sgt. 1st Herts Regt.
Hipgrave, F. Pte. 4th Beds Regt.
Hipgrave, J. L-Corp. 2nd Beds Regt.
Hipgrave, W. Pte. 1/5th Beds. Regt.
Hooker, F. Pte. (Corp) Beds Regt.
Humphreys, W. S. Trooper, 1st Herts Regt.
Hunt, A. G. 1st Class Stoker, Royal Navy
Hunt, F. W. Pte. 1/2nd Royal Fusiliers
Ingram, E. Pte. Suffolk Regt.
Ivory, W. J. Pte. 7th Norfolk Regt.
Johnson, G. W. Gunner, Machine Gun Corps.
Kitchener, C. Lt. Royal Garrison Artillery
Lancaster, A. C. Pte.10th Cheshire Regt.
Laughton, A. C. Pte. Beds Regt.
Lawrence, G. Pte. 75th Canadians
Lawrence, T. Pte. 75th Canadians
Loseby, A. E. Pte. 1st Herts Regt.
Martin, G. Pte. Beds Regt.
Massam, C. A. Pte. 3rd Beds Regt.
Matthews, J. E. Pte. Grenadiers Guards
Monk, J. H. Pte. 1st Beds Regt.
Moore, R. W. Pte. 1st Border Regt.
Munday, J. Pte. Essex Regiment
Nason, F. G. Pte. 4th Dorsetshire Regt.
Newman, F. Pte. 3rd Royal Fusiliers
Nicholson, G. E. Rifleman, South African Mounted Rifles.
Osborn, S. H. (DCM) Sgt. 1st Herts. Regt.
Page, D. Pte. Royal Marine Artillery
Page, E. J. A. L-Corp. Royal Eng.
Page, J. C. W. Pte. 1st Herts. Regt.
Pallett, J. W. Sgt. Beds. Regt.
Panter, G. M. Pte. 1/14th London Scottish Regt.
Parker, W. C. Signalman, Royal Navy

Parrott, F. A. Pte. 6th Sherwood Forresters
Parrott, H. J. Pte. Machine Gun Corps
Parrott, W. J. Sapper, Royal Engineers
Payne, J. Sgt. 13th Royal Berks Regt.
Pegram, A.R.H. Rifleman, Royal Irish Rifles
Penn, W. N. Pte. K. O. R. Lancs Regt.
Perkins, W. J. L-Corp. 1st Middx Regt.
Phillips, H.H. Lt. Leicestershire Regt.
Plume, F. W. Pte. Machine Gun corps.
Pollard, T. D. Pte. 2nd Beds Regt.
Powell, G. Corp. Herts Regt.
Powley, L. Pte. 8th Royal Fusiliers
Putterill, R. W. Pte. 6th Royal Berks Regt.
Randall, H. (DCM) Sgt, 1st Herts Regt.
Randal, W. J. L-Corp. Royal Eng.
Reid, G.P.N. Lt. Essex Yeomanry
Rice, G. Sgt. 18th Gloucester Regt.
Richardson, J. Sapper, Royal Eng.
Risebero, A. A. Q-M.Sgt. 1st Herts. Regt.
Riseboro, W.R.W. Pte. 4th Duke of Beds Regt.
Roberts, T. W. Pte. Royal Dublin Fus.
Scott, L. W. L-Corp. Machine Gun Corps.
Selway, S. J. Bombardier, Royal Marine Artillery
Sharp, C. G. Pte. 2nd Beds Regt.
Sharp. D. Pte. 4th Beds.Regt.
Skeggs, A. E. Pte. 6th Beds Regt.
Smith, A. Pte. 1/7th Manchester Regt.
Smith, A. G. Pte. Royal Garrison Art.
Smith, J. A. Pte. Machine Gun Corps.
Springett, F. R. Pte. 7th Sussex Regt.
Stallon, A. E. Pte. 1st Herts Regt.
Stallon, A. T. Pte. 8th Lincs Regt.
Stallon, W. Pte. 7th Beds Regt.
Starkey, J. A. 1st Air Mechanic, R.A.F.
Stockbridge, A. A. Pte. Herts Regt.
Stockbridge, C. G. Pte. Herts Regt.
Sunderland, R. Sapper, Royal Eng.
Taylor, C. G. Pte. 1st Herts Regt.
Tyler, A. E. Pte. 1st Herts Regt.
Tyler, Bertie (Albert) Pte. 1st Beds Regt.
Walker, A. W. Sgt. Royal Army Service Corps.
Walker, J. H. 2nd Lt. Royal Flying Corps.
Warren, H. V. Pte. 9th Royal Fus.
Webb, H. Corp. 1st Herts Regt.
Webster, G. T. Corp. K.O.Yorkshire Light Infantry.
Webster, G. V. Corp, Machine Gun Corps.
Welch, H. W. Pte. York & Lancs Regt.
Wren, G. J. Pte. 6th Royal Berks Regt.
Wren, R. C. Pte. 17th Royal Welsh Fus.
Wright, G. A. Pte. 1st Herts Regt.

The way in which the community came together to establish the town's memorial is reflected in similar events that were taking place throughout this country and overseas at this time. Whilst the plans for the memorial at the entrance to Hatfield Park were intended to commemorate all the men from the Hatfield district who had lost their lives as a result of the war, it was not surprising that the villages that formed part of the ancient Parish of Bishops Hatfield were keen to have their own memorial in their immediate locality. The people of Lemsford decided that their commemoration should take the form of a Celtic cross in Cornish granite, erected in the churchyard at St John's Church, close to the road, bearing the names of the 16 local men who had fallen. The work was carried out without delay and the memorial was unveiled at a service held on 20 July 1919. Accounts reveal that the ceremony took place in poor weather in the presence of a large gathering who watched as General the Earl of Cavan performed the unveiling.

Lemsford Memorial

LEMSFORD WAR MEMORIAL NAMES

F. Bunnage, Pte. Royal Marine Light Infantry.	F. W. Spriggs, Pte. Bedfordshire Regiment
D. Cochrane, Pte. Queen's Own Royal West Kent Regiment.	G. Spriggs, Pte. Hertfordshire Regiment 1st Bn.
H. E. Freeman, Pte.7th Bedfordshire Regiment*	W. J. Strong, Lieut.Lancaster Fusiliers 18th Bn.
R. W. Goodge, Gunner, Royal field Artillery	R. Tims, Rifleman,2/18th London Irish Rifles
J. Halsey, L/Corporal, Canadian Infantry, 49th Bn.	S. Walby, MM. Sgt. 2nd Bedfordshire Regiment
G. Hill, Pte. East Surrey Regiment	H.W. Welch, Pte. York & Lancaster Regiment*
E. Mardle, Pte. Royal Sussex Regiment	C. B. White, Pte. Royal Fusiliers
F. Mardle, Bombardier, Royal Field Artillery	C. Wren, Pte. 2nd Bedfordshire Regiment

*These two names also appear on the Hatfield Memorial

Two men with Lemsford connections as a result of their employment with Lord Mount Stephen at Brocket Hall are known to have lost their lives whilst serving in the army during the war but are not listed on any local memorials. However their names appear on the list of men from the Hatfield District on the St Albans Diocese Roll of Honour. They are:-

Private Herbert LEE   -   Suffolk Regiment
Private William RHODES   -   Bedfordshire Regiment

Similar preparations were being made at Hatfield Hyde where residents had expressed a wish that a local memorial should be erected to commemorate the men from Hatfield Hyde and Mill Green who had been lost (originally 18 names were identified but now there are 22 names on the War Memorial). The site chosen was "George's Corner" where three roads met. On the evening of Palm Sunday in April 1920, after a service of Evensong in "the Hyde Chapel" a large crowd gathered to see Lord Salisbury unveil the tall white cross of Portland Stone, with a plinth bearing the names of the local men who had been lost. The Cross was dedicated by the Rector and flowers were laid at the foot of the cross at the end of the ceremony. It is stated that the community had raised almost £100 which proved to be more than sufficient to cover the cost of the memorial.

Hatfield Hyde Memorial

HATFIELD HYDE MEMORIAL NAMES

A. Baker, Pte. Canadian Inf. British Colombia Regt.	F. W. Hunt, Pte. 1/2nd Royal Fusiliers
W. H. (or H. W.) Bray, Corporal Hertfordshire Regt.	W. J. Ivory. Pte. 7th Norfolk Regiment
A. Butterworth, Pte. Royal Army Service Corps.	C. Lankester (or A.C. Lancaster), Pte. 10th Cheshire Regt.
F. C. Cooper, Pte.1st Hertfordshire Regiment	G. Martin, Pte. Bedfordshire Regiment
G. E. Cooper, L/Corporal 23rd Middlesex Regiment	H. Peart. L/Corporal New Zealand Gun Battalion
W. J. Cooper, Pte. 8th Bedfordshire Regiment	L. W. Scott, L/Corporal Machine Gun Corps.
T. G. Griffin, Pte. 4th Bedfordshire Regiment	C. G. Sharp, Pte. 2nd Bedfordshire Regiment
D. Groom, Pte. 5th Royal Irish Fusiliers	D. Sharp, Pte. 4th Bedfordshire Regiment
J. Hipgrave, L/Corporal 2nd Bedfordshire Regiment	F. Springett, Pte. 7th Essex Regiment
F.Hooker, Corporal 8th Bedfordshire Regement	J. A. Starkey, 1st Air Mechanic, Royal Air Force
A.G. Hunt, 1st Class Stoker, Royal Navy	R. C. Wren, Pte. 17th Royal Welsh Fusiliers

All these names also appear on the Hatfield War Memorial, except L/Corporal H. Peart.

Turning to the southernmost part of the Rural District it must not be overlooked that there is another public war memorial in the form of a stone plaque mounted on the wall at the front of the Church of Ponsbourne St Mary in Newgate Street Village, bearing the names of ten local men who lost their lives in the conflict plus the names of 40 others who fortunately returned at the end of their war service. Unfortunately, the records of the arrangements for the installation of this memorial are incomplete but there is little doubt that Sir Edward Hildred Carlile of Ponsbourne Park would have played a major role in ensuring that the contribution of the local men was recognised in an appropriate way. Sir (Edward) Hildred Carlile was a very influential man in the community, a philanthropist who served for many years as MP for St Albans, including the period of the war.

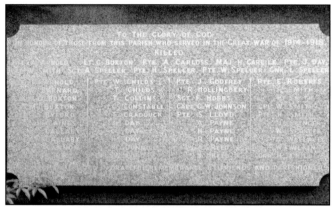

Ponsbourne & Newgate Street Memorial

PONSBOURNE/NEWGATE STREET WAR MEMORIAL NAMES

A. Arnold, Pte. Bedfordshire Regiment	W.T. Smith, Pte. L/Corporal, Bedfordshire Regiment
G. B. Buxton, Lieutenant, Royal Flying Corps.	A. C. Speller, Sergeant, 2nd Bedfordshire Regiment
A. Carloss. Pte. Royal Army Medical Corps.	H. J. Speller, Pte. Royal Engineers
E. H. H. Carlile. Major, Hertfordshire yeomanry	L. (W.) Speller, Gunner, Royal Field Artillery
J. Day, Pte. 1st Hertfordshire Regiment	W. J. Speller, Corporal, Machine Gun Corps

These 10 names all appear in the Hatfield "In Memoriam & Roll of Honour" Album but do not appear on the Hatfield War Memorial

A framed Roll of Honour scroll hanging in Ponsbourne St Mary Church lists all these men plus two others who lost their lives and whose names also appear on War Memorials in Hertford and Northaw respectively. The names of six other men with local connections are also listed on the Roll of Honour among the survivors.

Whilst the movement to erect memorials really took off once the fighting had ceased it is apparent that local communities had already been active in a less formal way, setting up local memorials to their fallen colleagues almost as soon as the casualties occurred and certainly whilst the battles were still raging.   A well-documented example of this took place in Newtown where local resident Mrs Royds led a campaign to recognise the sacrifice made by the men of Newtown and Roe Green.   Her efforts came to fruition towards the end of 1917 when the Rector led a service of hymns and prayers before unveiling a War Shrine, described as having a beautiful crucifix in the centre and a shelf for vases of flowers below. The shrine was fixed to the wall of the residence of Mrs Higgs in St Albans Road and contributions towards the cost had been collected from resident of Newtown, Roe Green and Astwick. Sadly in February 1919 the shrine was torn down and this led to a decision being made to restore the memorial with the names of all 46 men from the Newtown vicinity who lost their lives,

St Luke's Memorial

lettered in gold, and placed in St Luke's Church, where it remains today. The names of all these men appear on the Hatfield War Memorial.

Towards the end of 1919 a grant in excess of £200 was received from the United Services Fund which had been set up to care for the interests of ex-Servicemen. On receipt of this sum the Local Welfare Committee of the Fund resolved that the money should be donated to Hertford County Hospital where two Memorial Beds were then dedicated to local men who had given their lives during the years of conflict. In acknowledgment it was decided that brass plates should be installed above the beds with the following wording inscribed on them:-

From the Ex-Service Men of the Hatfield District
In Memory of
Their Comrades who fell in the Great War
1914-1919

The plaques are now displayed on the first floor waiting area of the hospital but there are now three such plaques which suggests that there may possibly have been a further donation from the same fund.

At a time when the nation wanted to remember their fallen colleagues it was understandable that throughout the country major employers and schools were keen to pay tribute to friends who were not able to return. A local example of this was Dagmar House School, situated at the junction of the

Dagmar House School Memorial

Lt. (Captain) John William Church Memorial

Great North Road and the St Albans Road, which at the time was a well-established fee paying and boarding school. Inevitably many of the old boys of the school served in the War and records show that 21 Old Dagmarians did not return. Four of the men lost were members of local families but others came from various parts of the country and some of them had almost certainly been

boarders at the school. So it was that on 19 January 1922 a ceremony was held in the Parish Church in the presence of many former Dagmarians and their Principal, Mr J. R. Sheehan-Dare, to give thanks to their fallen colleagues and to witness the unveiling of a marble tablet listing the 21 "fallen heroes". The tablet, bearing the school motto "Deo Adjuvante Non Timendum Est" (With God Assisting We Must Not Fear), was erected on the wall of the north side of the Nave, close to the pews where they would have worshipped as pupils. The brief service culminated with the unveiling of the tablet by the Bishop of St Albans, followed by a dedicatory prayer, the Last Post, two minutes silence, Reveille, the National Anthem and finally the hymn "For All the Saints".

Before the Dagmar ceremony took place other memorials had been erected in St Etheldreda's Parish Church. One of these was a plaque dedicated to Lieutenant (Captain) John William Church of the Hertfordshire Regiment who was killed in action on 30 March 1918. He was the elder son of Sir William Selby Church of Woodside. Several generations of the family had been prominent members of the local community. Sir William, who served as President of the Royal College of Physicians, and as a County Councillor, was Chairman of the Hatfield Rural District Council throughout the war years.

Another memorial, in the form of a white marble tablet, dedicated to members of the 4th Battalion of the Bedfordshire Regiment (Harts Militia), was unveiled in the Parish Church at around the same time. It was considered very appropriate to commemorate the men of the Militia in the town as they had often held their summer camp in Hatfield Park. The fact that these two memorials were installed in the Church in the autumn of 1920 demonstrates the deep feelings of loss that remained within the community for many years after the end of the war.

4th Battalion Bedfordshire Regiment (Harts Militia) Memorial

Exactly a year after the joyful peace celebrations the deep feelings of loss and thanks for the restoration of peace remained very strong among the public. This was demonstrated by the holding of a United Memorial Service on 18 July 1920. Organised by the Hatfield Branch of the Federation of Discharged Sailors and Soldiers, it took place on the North Front of Hatfield House in the presence of a crowd of approaching two thousand people. It had assembled at the station and processed through the town and up Fore Street, led by the Ware Silver Band, before entering the Park. Representatives of all the local services and organisations took part in the service which was conducted by Lord William Cecil, the Bishop of Exeter, accompanied by Lady Florence.

Mention has already been made among the Family Stories of the heavy personal loss sustained by Lord William Cecil, previously Rector at St Etheldreda's and his wife, Lady Florence who lost three sons in the conflict. Such a tragedy was worthy of suitable recognition within the Parish and Lord Salisbury took steps to commemorate the loss of his three nephews by arranging for the installation of a stained glass window in the north wall of the Nave. On the morning of Sunday 1 August 1920 the service of dedication was held in the presence of a full congregation on what was probably a unique occasion due to the presence of four Bishops including the Bishop of Exeter, the Bishop of St Albans, the Archbishop of Cape Town and the Bishop of Hankow

The Cecil Memorial Window

Christopher Whall designed the memorial window on the north wall of the nave near to the porch. The window is dedicated to the memory of three of the Cecil family and the inscription reads:-

"TO THE GLORY OF GOD AND IN MEMORY OF RUPERT EDWARD GASCOYNE CECIL BORN JANY 20TH 1895 KILLED IN ACTION JULY 11 1915 AND OF RANDLE WILLIAM GASCOYNE CECIL BORN NOVR 28TH 1889 KILLED IN ACTION DECR 1ST 1917 AND OF JOHN ARTHUR GASCOYNE CECIL BORN MARCH 28TH 1893 KILLED IN ACTION AUGUST 27TH 1918
I LOOK FOR THE RESURRECTION OF THE DEAD AND THE LIFE OF THE WORLD TO COME".

The window consists of three lights. The window was presented in 1920 by James, Fourth Marquess of Salisbury, in memory of his three nephews. Their father was Lord William Cecil, then Bishop of Exeter who had previously been rector at Hatfield. The three angels in the work represent "Trial and Sacrifice" (crown of thorns), "Victory and Triumph" (resurrection and torch) and "Christian Duty" (baptism of the infant). The red seraphim in the tracery above represent "Divine Love" and the blue seraphim represent "Divine Wisdom.

(Wikipedia & UK Inventory of War Memorials)